Declaration
of a
HERETIC

Jeremy Rifkin is the President of the Foundation on Economic Trends based in Washington DC. He is the author of eight books: *Common Sense II, Own Your Own Job, The North will Rise Again* (with Randy Barber), *Who should Play God?, The Emerging Order,* the best-selling *Entropy* (all three written with Ted Howard), *Algeny* (in collaboration with Nicanor Perlas) and *Declaration of a Heretic*.

Declaration *of a* HERETIC

Jeremy Rifkin

Routledge & Kegan Paul
Boston, London, Melbourne and Henley

First published in 1985
by Routledge & Kegan Paul plc

9 Park Street, Boston, Mass. 02108, USA

14 Leicester Square, London WC2H 7PH, England

464 St Kilda Road, Melbourne,
Victoria 3004, Australia and

Broadway House, Newtown Road,
Henley on Thames, Oxon RG9 1EN, England

Set in Palatino
by Columns of Reading
and printed in the United States of America

Library of Congress Cataloging in Publication Data

Rifkin, Jeremy.

Declaration of a heretic.
Bibliography: p.
1. Nuclear energy. 2. Genetic engineering.
3. Science–Social aspects. I. Title.
TK9153.R54 1985 174'.95 85-2490

British Library CIP data also available

ISBN 0-7102-0709-3 (cloth)
ISBN 0-7102-0710-7 (paper)

For my stepchildren, Joshua and Anie, who have taught me so many wonderful things and brought so much joy into my life . . . and for their generation.

I would like to give special thanks to my wife, Donna, for conceiving the final outline for the book and for encouraging me not to abandon the project. This book would probably not have been written were it not for her insistence that the ideas needed to be published.

I would like to thank Nicanor Perlas for his help in compiling the Reading List for *Declaration of a Heretic*. I would also like to thank my editor, Stratford Caldecott, for both his encouragement and commitment to this book.

Contents

Preface

I have been accused of being opposed to scientific inquiry, academic freedom and, worst of all, the march of progress. I have been castigated as an obstructionist, a spoiler, a man dedicated to slowing, retarding or halting the further advances of the human race. Occasionally a scientist, corporate leader or policy maker will cast doubt on my temporal sanity, insisting that my real desire is to turn back the clock of time; how far back is often determined by the ire of the assailant. Some have said that I am really a romantic at heart and believe that the best of all possible worlds is an idyllic pastoral or agrarian order, unencumbered by the hissing, cranking sounds of the industrial machine. Others have suggested that my opposition to the scientific and technological fruits of civilization runs still deeper, and that, if I had my way, the wheel itself might never have been allowed to roll across this earthly terrain. There are even those who remain convinced that I could only be truly satisfied were humanity to retreat all the way back to its earliest state, that of the noble savage, propertyless, homeless and virtually undifferentiated from its surroundings.

I have taken pen to hand in this declaration in an attempt to present my views on such things as the nature of progress, the scope of scientific inquiry, the legitimate uses of technology and the appropriate forms of economic organization.

At the outset, let me say that I consider this exercise to be far more than a personal affair. I would like to think that what I have to say represents, in some small way, the thinking of many other people who have begun seriously to question some of the underlying assumptions of the "Age of Progress."

If there is a single defining characteristic that distinguishes the modern age, it is the unqualified faith we have in the ability of science and technology to address and resolve the great issues of our times. So slavish is our devotion to the "scientific world view" that whenever the faintest hint of criticism is leveled at the introduction of a new technological breakthrough, the scientific establishment is likely to accuse the critics of stifling freedom of inquiry and obstructing progress. I have written this essay to express my solidarity with all of those who have felt themselves to be on the receiving end of such declaratory judgements.

The central message of this declaration is that it is possible to be in favor of progress, freedom of inquiry and the advancement of consciousness, and still be opposed to essential elements of the prevailing scientific and technological world view. In this essay, I have suggested that "the scientific world view" we have come to accept as an article of faith is but one approach to reality, an approach whose built-in flaws and limitations are becoming increasingly apparent with each passing day. It is my fervent hope that the next generation will come to realize that the human consciousness is capable of choosing many very different approaches to knowledge, and that the human mind is capable of choosing many alternative futures. We stifle freedom of inquiry and undermine the great potential of human consciousness only when we steadfastly refuse to entertain new ways of re-imagining our world.

This short essay is intended as both a challenge to the orthodox approach to the pursuit of knowledge we have come to accept, and a call for charting new directions for the human consciousness in the years to come.

We need to redefine our notions of progress, reshape our ideas about the nature of scientific inquiry, redefine our relationship to tools, and redesign the conceptual basis of economic activity. It is imperative that we set our clocks forward, that we expand our consciousness, that we refire our imagination, that we rekindle our expectations, and that we recast our vision. For some, such thoughts will no doubt be looked on as sheer heresy. For others, such thoughts raise the prospect of a fresh beginning and a renewed sense of hope. It is to the latter that I address my appeal.

Introduction

Introduction

There have been two great scientific discoveries in this century. In 1942 American physicists unleashed the first sustained nuclear reaction catapulting the world into the Atomic Age. A decade later two young molecular biologists discovered the double helix, ushering in the dawn of the Genetics Age.

According to the conventional wisdom both of these technological breakthroughs have brought both benefits and costs. On balance, however, the world is better off, in two respects, for their having been introduced. First, these discoveries have increased our knowledge about ourselves and the world we live in and brought us closer to understanding the basic truths of our existence. Second, these basic discoveries have given birth to a new generation of tools that have made our lives more secure and the future more hopeful. This then, is the conventional wisdom of our time.

So convinced are we of the rightness of our point of view on this matter that, in the many years that have elapsed since these two marvels were presented to our species for inspection, not even the faintest murmur of protest has been recorded that might imply disapproval of the discoveries themselves or the mentality underlying them. That is not to say that there hasn't been spirited dialogue on "how" these discoveries are to be employed. Rather, there has not been the slightest hint of a suggestion that perhaps we ought not to make use of them at all, under any circumstances.

To cast these discoveries aside. To let languish the concepts that gave rise to them. To abandon the line of intellectual thought that led up to them. To say no to the human motivation that inspired them. For the true believers, the staunch upholders of the existing orthodoxy, such thoughts qualify as heresy.

Of course heresy is not a new phenomenon. Every civilization in history has had its fair share of heretics, those unwilling or unable to accept the governing world view of the culture. The most celebrated example of heresy in the modern era is the often cited confrontation between the scientist Galileo and the church establishment.

Galileo's challenge extended well beyond the question of astronomical facts. If that were all that was being contested, he might have remained, to this day, a rather minor footnote to our intellectual history. Galileo's crime was far more serious. He was questioning the Church's world view, its underlying premise about the nature of reality and existence. It was the Church's approach to knowledge, the way it viewed the search for truth that Galileo inevitably had to grapple with. The great debate between Galileo and the Church was over competing world views, and only secondarily over disputed astronomical facts.

Today's faith system is the scientific world view. Today's Church is the scientific establishment. It is the Nobel laureates and other scientific functionaries who serve as the defenders of the faith, the standard bearers of the world view of Western civilization. Today's orthodoxy is steeped in the catechism of the Enlightenment. The apostles of truth are no longer Peter, Paul, John, Mark and Luke. They are Bacon, Descartes, Newton, Locke and Darwin. If there is a universal faith today, a faith that supersedes political ideologies, economic philosophies and religious doctrines, it is most assuredly the faith we place in the scientific world view. Its central assumptions have become dogma. We have all been baptized in the precepts of the scientific method. We have all learned to pay homage to the prelates of the scientific academy: the hordes of experts who discover and decipher the "truth" for us.

The first sustained nuclear reaction and the discovery of the double helix are products of the scientific world view. As such they represent a unique way of thinking, a special approach to understanding the world that is characteristic of a specific historical moment. Had Western civilization entertained a radically different world view, it is very likely that these two discoveries might never have materialized. They might have remained an unformed possibility, never to become part of the consciousness of the race.

If this thought is hard to imagine, it is perhaps because we are so enmeshed in the set of assumptions that make up the modern scientific world view that we are unable to fathom the possibility that a different set of assumptions might have led us to a radically different technological reality today.

So unshakeable is our faith in the principles of modern science that we consider any serious criticism of its central tenets to be highly irrational and extremely dangerous. Only a madman would dare challenge what has long since been accepted as gospel. Our civilization is so firmly entrenched in the scientific doctrine of the Enlightenment that it will not easily tolerate any direct challenge to its underlying assumptions.

But challenge we must. The future of our civilization, our species and our planet now hangs precariously in the balance. The scientific world view and the technologies it has generated have taken our world to the very edge of earthly existence, and now we face the prospect that the future itself might be annulled in our lifetime. Certainly now is the time for us to reassess our world view, to ask basic questions about the assumptions we rely on to organize and understand the world we live in.

The best place to begin such an inquiry is to ask what kind of thoughts might be considered heretical if placed before the tribunal of established scientific opinion today. For example, is it heresy to suggest that the particular approach to knowledge we have given our allegiance to, for these past several hundred years, is alienating us even further from the natural world we so desperately seek to understand? Is it heresy to suggest that the fruits of the scientific world view have been a mixed blessing, often causing more harm than good? Is it heresy to suggest that the two great scientific discoveries of this century provide us with inordinate power over the forces of nature and ought not to be used? Is it heresy to suggest that alternative approaches to science and technology are indeed possible to contemplate and act upon? Heresy perhaps. But, it is also possible that the scientific world view of the Enlightenment has run its course, and that by continuing to adhere unqualifiedly to its assumptions, we make the world a less secure and more dangerous place to live in.

We are long past due for a discussion about first principles. To question the thinking of our age, to open up the door to new challenges for the human intellect: this is the single most pressing concern on the human agenda as we turn the corner into the second millennium AD.

In the final analysis, it is our willingness to entertain a revolutionary change in the way we think about each other and the world that will determine whether there will be a future. Nothing short of such a transformation can hope to reverse our present course.

Part I

The Split Atom

1
A Gift from the Gods

It began with an explosion. Suddenly the black vacuous caverns of space were alight. Fire swept through the heavens, splashing its imprint on the universe. Torrential and blinding, this raging force careened through the cosmic reaches filling nothingness with motion and substance.

On its journey through the cosmos, this great firestorm left parts of itself behind. These fiery oases, these isolated lights spanning the heaven, were like markers chronicling the path of that first wind of fire.

Over eons of time these pockets of raging fire consumed themselves, spitting out their essence, creating a village of moltenous satellites. The satellites began to cool. They took shape and form. They became planets and asteroids and moons.

Somewhere half hidden in the litter of a hundred million fires, somewhere tucked away in the ashen debris that dots the cosmic landscape, somewhere in the shadow of a sprinkle of lights that seems never to end, lies a tiny speck, a little globe spinning in ritualistic progression along a well worn trajectory. This is Earth, born in the violent aftermath of the first great cosmic firestorm. . . .

The earth was a fiery remnant that cooled off. The gods took notice of this cold, barren outpost and decided that it would be an appropriate environment for fashioning life. Two gods, Epimetheus and Prometheus, were dispatched to earth. Their mission was to provide all of the newly designed creatures with their proper qualities. By the time they came to human beings, Prometheus noticed that Epimetheus had already distributed all the qualities at his disposal to the rest of the plants and animals. Not wanting to leave human beings totally unprotected, Prometheus stole the mechanical arts and fire from the gods and gave them to men and women. With these acquisitions, humanity acquired knowledge that originally belonged only to the gods.

Fire, says Lewis Mumford, provided human beings with light, power, and heat – three basic things necessary for survival. Commenting on the role of fire in human development, Mumford concludes that it "counts as man's unique technological achievement: unparalleled in any other species." With fire, human beings could melt down the inanimate world of nature and reshape it into a world of pure utilities. As historian Theodore Wertime of the Smithsonian Institution observes:

> *there is almost nothing that is not brought to a finished state by means of fire. Fire takes this or that sand, and melts it, according to the locality, into glass, steel, cinnabar, lead of one kind or another, pigments or drugs. It is fire that smelts ore into copper, fire that burns stone (cement) which causes the blocks in buildings to cohere.*

The age of pyrotechnology began in earnest around 3000 BC in the Mediterranean and Near East, when people shifted from the exclusive use of muscle power in shaping inanimate nature to the use of fire. Pounding, squeezing, breaking, mashing and grinding began to play second fiddle to fusing, melting, soldering, forging and burning. By refiring the cold remains of what was once a fireball itself, human beings began the process of recycling the crust of the planet into a new home for themselves.

Our history is the history of our consuming relationship to fire. We are truly a promethean creature. Armed with fire, we have recast the face of the earth in our own image. With the aid of fire technology we have placed ourselves in the role of master over the rest of creation. Fire has given us control over our own environment and each other. We have long been enthralled with its power. Unlike all the other species we alone are unafraid to commune with it, to use it, to nurture it.

On December 2, 1942, after countless millennia of experimentation with fire, a tiny band of scientists huddled beneath the bleachers of a football stadium on the campus of the University of Chicago. On that day they unleashed the first sustained atomic reaction. They presented their new gift to the world. We now have assembled a concentration of fire power so potent, that even the god Prometheus might entertain second thoughts about the wisdom of his initial act of charity.

With the nuclear bomb, with tens of thousands of nuclear bombs, we have enough fire power at our disposal to re-enact the origins of existence. All we need do is drop the products of our own handiwork upon the earth and in one blinding moment we can relight the original fireball that was the earth at its birth. We can turn earth to fire, we can turn the mountains and rivers and lands into molten liquid, we can whiten the heavens with a flash reminiscent of our beginnings. We have come full cycle. After ages and eons and epochs we come to the crossroad of our own earthly existence. We now have the power to come back to the very beginning of our story. But this time there is no assurance that the fury of death will be followed by the exaltation of rebirth.

2

The Journey from Eden to Armageddon

Most historians prefer to think of the nuclear bomb as a by-product of World War II. They credit its development to a handful of scientists, politicians and military tacticians working in tandem to produce the ultimate weapon: a weapon that could guarantee victory for the Allied powers. If only it were that easy to explain away the emergence of such overwhelming lethality. It would be reassuring to be able to pinpoint responsibility so neatly. We could isolate the key personalities involved at the center of the command structure, and evaluate the wisdom of their decision on the basis of the geopolitical context in which they were operating. Unfortunately it is not that easy. The bomb does not owe its existence to World War II, only its birthday. Had there not been a war, we would still be faced with the bomb today.

Preparation for the bomb began well before World War II, well before $E=MC^2$, well before the twentieth century. The bomb is not a circumstance, a situation or even an event. It is a culmination. It is not just the work of an Einstein, an Oppenheimer or a Teller. It is the work of the collective consciousness of the human race. Preparation for the bomb began back at the very beginning of time, at that very moment when the human mind took its first tentative step into the realm of consciousness. The bomb belongs to all of us. Its inspiration lies deeply embedded in the psyche of the race. Its genius is traceable to the countless excursions of the human mind over the ages.

The story of the bomb begins with the story of our species and that story begins back in the garden of Eden on the sixth day. On that day God created Adam and Eve from the dust and ashen debris of the great cosmic firestorm. And to these two beautiful creatures God gave dominion over the fish of the sea, the fowl of the air and over every living thing that dwelt within the lush green garden of paradise. In the garden Adam and Eve were without want. Their every need was provided for. They felt no anxiety, no concern for their future. There was no fear of death in Paradise. They were secure. In return for their good fortune God only asked that they not eat from the tree of knowledge, because to do so would be to claim their earthly independence of God. Armed with knowledge they could assert their authority over God's and begin to wrest from him power over the rest of creation.

God's admonition proved ineffective. The serpent beguiled Eve into eating the fruit from the tree. Eve in turn, seduced Adam. Together they fell from grace, plunging headlong into the world of human consciousness. The history of consciousness begins in the Garden of Eden with that fateful first act of defiance against the Lord Almighty.

When Adam and Eve disobeyed, God meted out the supreme punishment. He made Adam and Eve mortal and banished them from Paradise. Because they were now conscious, having eaten from the tree of knowledge, they would be forever conscious of their own mortality. From that time on, they and their heirs would live in constant fear of their own impending death. In expelling the pair from the garden, the lord Jehovah admonished them that the future of their kind would be fraught with insecurity. Life would be harsh and exacting and without reprieve. An ever-present anxiety would pervade the human experience and that anxiety would be the awareness of our own mortality.

The entire history of the human experience, from the time Adam and Eve stepped outside of the garden, has been marked by a single overriding drive: to recapture the security that was lost when we were expelled from the garden. And so it came to pass that Adam and Eve and their children and their descendants went forth into a hostile world determined to survive, and to overcome the obstacles God had set in their way.

Left to their own devices, Adam and Eve used the one

attribute they had expropriated to set them apart from the other species, the ability to acquire knowledge. This unique quality became their rod and their staff. They would regain the security that they had been deprived of by using their consciousness to erect their own garden, their own earthly Paradise. (In anthropological terms, the fall from grace represents the transition from a participatory pre-historic consciousness reflective of the early hunter-gatherer mode of existence to an historical consciousness indicative of the first great Western civilizations at Sumer and Mesopotamia.)

To achieve its goal of security, humanity has used knowledge, the gift it plucked from the very special tree in the center of Paradise, as its salvation. Knowledge is defined as a decrease in uncertainty or an increase in probability, which is a more technical way of saying that knowledge is the ability "to know," to predict, to foretell one's own destiny. From the very beginning, human beings have used their consciousness to gain knowledge of the world around them so that they could control their fate and replace God here on earth. Total knowledge implies complete awareness from beginning to end of every single unfolding event that will ever occur in the world. To become God is to become all knowing.

It's no wonder that after expelling Adam and Eve from Paradise, God hurriedly erected a defense perimeter around the garden lest the pair sneak back in and head for the other special tree in the earthly grove, the tree of everlasting life. Armed with the power to know all things and with everlasting life, Adam and Eve would become just like God.

God was not about to let that happen. So the gates to Paradise were locked shut. Two frightened semi-naked creatures huddled outside the gates, left to ponder their own demise. Finally, they rose to their feet, dusted themselves off, took a last furtive glance back at the garden which was once their domain, and then hesitantly set off into the wilderness in hopes of recapturing the security they had left behind.

From that time forward, the human species has never once wavered from a single-minded pre-occupation with security. We yearn for the security we once enjoyed in the garden. We are desperate to overcome our own mortality, to rid ourselves of the constant nagging realization of our own precarious and limited existence. We want our future to be secure, our life to be secure. We want to live on in perpetuity.

Our desire to perpetuate ourselves has spawned an insatiable appetite; a lust to manipulate and expropriate the environment around us. We have come to believe that by devouring more and more of the earth's resources, including other living things, we will somehow succeed in cheating death, in transcending our own mortality. So we have zealously used that precious gift of consciousness to develop a certain kind of knowledge; a controlling knowledge, an usurping knowledge. We have sought knowledge of our environment so that we might exercise control over it. We have come to believe that if we can eventually master every single aspect of our earthly world, we can at last feel secure. We can rise above the vagaries of physical existence and recapture the immortality we once enjoyed in those early days in the garden.

It is this consuming drive for security that has finally led to the ultimate exercise of power over the environment, the development of the nuclear bomb. We built the bomb to gain a measure of security. We continue to manufacture bigger and better bombs in order to maintain our security. The bomb represents the final victory in our long journey to gain control over the forces of nature and each other. It is an embodiment of the consciousness of the species: a consciousness that began on that first day of exile outside the gates of paradise.

If the bomb is the ultimate exercise of power, it has also become the ultimate source of embarrassment for the species. Our young people are beginning to ask us why we are building bigger and better bombs. They want to know why we are so incapable of extricating ourselves from a journey that is edging us closer to the apocalypse. If the truth be known, the honest answer to the question is "we know no other way." That's because, in the long history of human experience, we have trained our mind to pursue one kind of knowledge, the knowledge of control. We have believed that the more power we exercise, the more secure we become. This kind of controlling knowledge is expressed in the kinds of tools we have fashioned to interact with our environment and each other. Our technologies have reflected our desire to exercise power. In this context, the bomb emerges as the most successful technology we have ever conceived. Therefore, if we are to hope to understand our relationship to the bomb, we must begin by understanding the set of assumptions we have long entertained about the notions of power and security. It is these assumptions that have given rise to the nuclear phalanx, and that continue to feed the proliferating arms race.

While our attitudes about power and security are rooted in our ancient past, their most recent incarnation can be traced to a constellation of ideas that took shape several hundred years ago as Western Europe rose from its long agricultural past to pioneer the beginnings of the industrial era. It is these ideas of the European enlightenment that hold sway over the totality of our modern way of life, permeating every aspect of our social existence, including our military existence. Because our military and social values are inspired by the same set of philosophical assumptions, it is virtually impossible to entertain any discussion of nuclear weapons and nuclear warfare without also discussing the values and goals of the civilization as well. The same set of basic assumptions that we apply in the day-to-day operations of our society we apply to the development of our military objectives.

No doubt some among us believe that our culture has established two different sets of standards, one governing our activity as a society, the other governing our military defenses. In reality, there is no evidence whatsoever to corroborate such a schizophrenic diagnosis. Our military attitudes reflect our societal attitudes, and that is exactly why it is so difficult for us to contemplate the idea of disarming our weapons. To do so would require that we also take a deep probing look at the values that govern the affairs of our society, with an eye to disarming them as well.

Painful as such a prospect might be, there is no easy shortcut to disarmament that will allow us to bypass a discussion of the underlying assumptions that govern our day-to-day life as a people.

3

The Nuclear World View

We live by a set of intellectual constructs first articulated by a handful of European scholars several hundred years ago at the dawn of the modern era. Their ideas about the nature of "man" and the nature of "security" continue to influence our conceptions of the world today. If we are to understand the current nuclear crisis, we need to begin with an examination of the ideas that have led up to it. Those ideas begin with Francis Bacon.

One of the architects of the modern world view, Bacon wrote a small tract in 1620 called *Novum Organum* which laid out an approach to knowledge which we still hold to today. Bacon chastized earlier scholars who were interested in asking the simple why of things. Bacon was far more concerned with the how of things. Knowledge is important, he claimed, to the extent that it can be useful. Bacon saw knowledge as a tool for gaining control over the environment. He canonized the idea that "knowledge is power." Bacon looked to the day when the human store of knowledge would be sufficient to "subdue and overcome the necessities and miseries of humanity."

To advance this lofty goal, Bacon proclaimed that a new method for dealing with the world was called for; one that could "enlarge the bounds of human empire, to the effecting of all things possible." The new method Bacon alludes to is the "scientific" method, an approach that could separate the observer from the observed and provide a neutral forum for the development of "objective knowledge." According to Bacon, objective knowledge would allow people to take "command over things natural – over bodies, medicine, mechanical powers and infinite others of this kind."

Every school child is weaned on Bacon's scientific method. From the time we are first able to form a conception, we are informed that there is, in fact, an objective world out there whose secrets can be discovered and exploited to advance human ends. We are encouraged to create distance between ourselves and the world, to detach ourselves so that we can sever our natural relationships with things and turn them into objects for manipulation.

The scientific method is the penultimate expression of the approach to knowledge we have come to believe in. It reflects our consuming passion for predictability and order. We have transformed all of physical reality into a giant testing site and then attempted to discover predictable patterns of behavior that can be exploited over and over in such a way as to enhance our control over the forces of nature. The more successful we are at imperializing our environment, the more secure we feel. The long history of Western consciousness, which reached its zenith with the flowering of the Baconian revolution, can be summarized as follows: Knowledge is power, power is control, control is security.

While Francis Bacon provided a methodological approach for increasing our control over the environment, it was the ideas of René Descartes, Isaac Newton, John Locke, Adam Smith and Charles Darwin that laid the foundation for the new earthly garden. These learned men, these other architects of the modern world view, were in search of a set of operating principles that could provide the human family with the security it yearned for. Their prescriptions for ordering society and the physical world have passed down through eight generations and continue to animate the public life of our nation today. We measure the effectiveness of our own security by how well it coheres to the principles set forth by these men of yesterday: not only our private and public security, our political and economic security, but also our national and military security as well. To understand the arguments of these scholars, is to understand the philosophy that underlies our current national defense posture and our nuclear arms policy.

Bacon provided us with a new method for organizing the

environment, but it was René Descartes that gave us the tools. According to Descartes, if we strip the universe of all of the non-rational qualities we have ascribed to it, we find that it is, in its essence, a mathematical proposition. By using mathematics as our primary form of knowledge, Descartes claimed that it would be possible to elicit "true results in every subject."

Descartes was passionately committed to the idea that mathematics could unlock the secrets of nature and thus make human beings rulers of the cosmos. In fact, Descartes was so enamored with the power of mathematics, that he was simply unable to make room in his newly found world view for any considerations that were unquantifiable. "To speak freely," he said, "I am convinced that it (mathematics) is a more powerful instrument of knowledge than any other that has been bequeathed to us by human agency, as being the source of all things." Believing, like his predecessors, that knowledge is indeed power, Descartes summed up the great import of his newly discovered set of mathematical tools. "Give me extension and motion," he said, "and I will construct the universe."

Such bravado quickly led to a basic reappraisal of God's role in the affairs of history. If the universe ran by precise mathematical principles, and those principles could be discovered and used to control every aspect of physical reality, then what need was there of God in the new scheme of things? God was gradually eased out of the frame of world history. As he was being shuffled aside, Descartes and his contemporaries were quick to praise him for being the supreme architect who had designed the mathematical principles of the cosmic theater.

By redefining the world in mathematical terms, Descartes drained it of colours, feelings and every other non-quantifiable consideration. What was left was pure matter, devoid of any meaning.

Of course, the universe can lack any real sense of meaning and still be jumping with activity. And that's where Isaac Newton comes in. Newton animated Descartes' mathematical universe with three laws that he claimed governed all activity in the physical world. According to Newton, "A body at rest remains at rest and a body in motion remains in uniform motion in a straight line unless acted upon by an external force;

the acceleration of a body is directly proportional to the applied force and in the direction of the straight line in which the force acts; and for every force there is an equal and opposite force in reaction."

As a result of Newton's discoveries, Europeans began to perceive the universe as a giant mechanical construct operating by well formulated laws of matter in motion. In fact, it was not long before this new mechanical view of nature began to serve as a metaphor for redefining the totality of existence. It became fashionable among scholars to use mechanical terminology to explain and rationalize every aspect of life, including the affairs governing society.

Here was a new picture of the world emerging. Future generations would increasingly come to view their physical surroundings in mathematical and mechanical terms. By separating and then eliminating all of the qualities of life from the quantities of which they are a part, these philosophers of the modern world view were left with a sterile universe made up of simple matter in motion.

It was a short journey from the world as pure matter to the world of pure materialism. That journey was mapped out for future generations by two great philosophers, John Locke and Adam Smith.

Locke was anxious to find a way to order the activity of society to conform with the new mathematical and mechanical principles that Descartes and Newton claimed ordered the universe. Locke discovered an organizing principle in society that he believed was compatible with the new impersonal, detached, objective, rational, non-feeling universe of Bacon, Descartes and Newton. If the world is made up of isolated bits of matter in motion, each responsible only for its own perpetuation, then a similar standard must govern individual behavior. Locke concluded that each individual was like an isolated bit of matter in the universe with no other goal than to perpetuate itself. In a world that had already been reduced to pure material, Locke introduced a philosophy of pure materialism. According to Locke, if each individual is only concerned with maximizing his own material self-interest, then the proper role of government is to insure that the forces of nature are brought under control and harnessed so that each member of society could amass as much wealth as humanly possible. "The negation of nature," Locke contended, "is the way toward happiness."

Given Locke's premise about the nature of human beings, it's not hard to understand why he considered it a duty to expropriate as much of nature's resources as could be managed. Locke was so convinced that material security could only be won by exercising power and control over the environment that he came to view nature in its unmolested state as little more than idle waste. According to Locke, nature only becomes valuable when we harness it for our own ends.

Locke established a new political context that was congenial with the new universe people found themselves in. It was Adam Smith, however, who provided the economic rationale for this new way of thinking about the world. Smith argued that it is only by each individual attempting to maximize his own material advantage that the common good of society is advanced. While at first blush, it might well seem contradictory to assume that individual greed could ever prove beneficial to the welfare of others, Smith put forth a justification for this line of thinking that still retains its currency even today. According to Smith:

> *Every individual is continually exerting himself to find out the most advantageous employment for whatever capital he can command. It is his own advantage, indeed, and not that of society which he has in view. But the study of his own advantage naturally, or rather necessarily, leads him to prefer that employment which is most advantageous to society.*

Smith claimed to have discovered a natural law, the "invisible hand," which he said automatically regulated the supply and demand of scarce resources among all the members of society. According to Smith, an adequate knowledge of the workings of this law would insure greater power over the forces of nature and greater material security for the individual and the society.

In the short span of two hundred years or so, Western society was introduced to a new method for organizing the world, a new set of conceptual tools for getting the job done and a new political and economic philosophy to rationalize the new scheme of things. The only thing still needed to secure this view of the world was a new explanation of the origins of life that would be compatible with the rest of the paradigm. Charles Darwin provided the missing link.

Darwin looked into nature and saw the same mechanistic principles that Descartes and Newton used to define the universe and that Locke and Smith used to reorder society. According to Darwin, a law of nature insured the steady development of life from the simplest single-celled organism to contemporary man and woman. This law of nature, which Darwin says he discovered from careful observation of sheep breeding, is called "natural selection." According to this law, new biological modifications are continually presenting themselves with the birth of every new organism. Some of these changes are harmful to the survival of the organism, some are beneficial. Darwin argued that it is just a matter of pure luck whether an organism is blessed or cursed at birth. Chance not withstanding, the law of natural selection insures that the organism best able to take advantage of the opportunity presented by a potentially beneficial modification will enhance its ability to survive and therefore produce more offspring that will also survive.

According to the law of natural selection, the story of evolution is a story of rank opportunism and utilitarian self-interest. These are the overriding principles that govern the very fabric of life. In the long history of biological advancement, progress is measured by the ability of each succeeding species to better utilize scarce resources more effectively than its predecessor, thus insuring its own self-perpetuation and its heirs.

For Darwin, maximizing control over the environment becomes the *sine qua non* in nature as in society. Darwin, of course, believed that the human being is, by far, the most successful of all the species in controlling its environment because of its superior brain power. While other animals might exceed us in brute force or speed, the human mind gives us the edge, so far as natural selection is concerned, because it provides us with a superior means of exercising power and control over our surroundings.

The philosophers of the Enlightenment provided us with a radical new way of looking at the world. Their new perspective was accompanied by a new value orientation as well. The new value was efficiency, and society embraced it with an almost religious zeal, determined to make it the measure of all human activity.

If a scholar from another time period in human history were to inquire as to what has been the biggest single change in human relations in the past two centuries, the answer would not be the electrification of the social environment or the urbanization of the planet or the advent of mass communication. All of these things, though profoundly unsettling to traditional patterns of behavior, are only manifestations of a more deep-seated change in human values. For the first time in recorded history, a new value has emerged, and in a very short period of time it has effectively eclipsed every other deeply held traditional value that the human species has entertained over the ages. The value is efficiency, and in less than eight generations it has risen from obscure origins to become the one universally held value that cuts across all ideologies and geographic boundaries.

Today we measure both ourselves and our technology by how well both meet the standards prescribed by efficiency. Efficiency has become so integral to every part of our lives, that we are incredulous when informed that it has not always been the central reference point for gauging the merit and worth of most human endeavors.

If there is an overriding social mandate today, it is to be efficient. If there is one agreed upon approach for organizing the relationships between people and their environment it is efficiency. Efficiency is both a method and a value. As a method, efficiency conditions the human mind to eliminate all values and considerations that might in any way pose an obstacle to the complete maximization of the age-old equation: knowledge = power = control = security. It is true that in our long history as a species, many cultures have ensconsed this primary equation as the central theme of their sociality, but with this difference. Pre-modern societies allowed for a periodic reprieve from the incessant pursuit of control over the environment. Respites in the form of religious sacrifices, expiation rituals and death and rebirth celebrations provided a release, a surrendering of control, a momentary lapse in which the collective mind of the community could rest from its drive to power.

Efficiency introduces a wholly new orientation. A premium is placed on constant improvement of the knowledge, power, control, security equation. There is no room for marginal concerns, no allowance for other values to come into play. Efficiency is no longer one among many values we hold. It has become a mandate. Finding more effective ways of controlling our environment has become the overriding, ever-present reality.

We seek to make our technology more efficient, ourselves more efficient and our society more efficient. Efficiency as both a method and a value reorients the whole of the human experience to one end: total mastery of the physical world. To be efficient means to optimize both the speed and quantity of our expropriation, and to minimize the time and participation necessary to secure the objects of our attention.

Today, the individual mind and the collective consciousness of the species gives more thought to efficiency than any other single pursuit. We have streamlined ourselves, our tools and our culture to make one last surging bid for mastery over the earth and all that inhabits it. Efficiency has become both our mental roadmap and our succor. The more efficient we become, the more secure we feel. Efficiency and security have become virtually interchangeable.

4

Disarming our Way of Life

In surveying the ideas of the great philosophers of the modern era, one is struck by how current their thinking still seems to be. Though most of us are barely familiar with their names, we are well versed in their views on the nature of human beings, society and the world we live in. Their views are our views. In fact, their ideas are so deeply integrated into our entire socializing experience that we have come to accept their way of thinking uncritically. This is no less true when it comes to our attitudes about military preparedness and defense policies. While our strategic war planners don't sit around the war room asking themselves how the architects of the modern world view would have approached the various military options available, they do the next best thing. They effectively incorporate the essential assumptions of these seminal thinkers into the rubric of their day-to-day operations. In this sense, our diplomats and generals are little more than actors in a drama that was scripted back in the seventeenth, eighteenth and nineteenth centuries by a gifted club of scholars who believed, without reservation, that they had discovered the formula for guaranteeing the security of the human family. Every position paper, every briefing, every public pronouncement, every strategic move and counter move, every technological advance in our military program remains consistent with the reflections and declarations of the great architects of the modern world view.

Our ideas about security are bound up in the world view we have inherited: a world view rooted in the very beginning of human consciousness, and expressed in its most up to date version in the words of men like Francis Bacon, René Descartes, Isaac Newton, John Locke, Adam Smith and Charles Darwin. It is their ideas that are put out on the conference table during disarmament negotiations, and it is their ideas that are presented to the American public to justify and explain our nuclear policy.

Indeed, what makes the present nuclear crisis appear so intractable, so utterly irreconcilable are the ideas about security we share as a culture. It is these very ideas that seem only to bring us closer and closer to the crossroads of our own history as a species.

If we feel hopeless and resigned, it is because we are tormented by a dilemma without parallel in the annals of the human sojourn. We seek security: our own, our children's, our culture's, our civilization's, our species'. Yet, every initiative we undertake to resolve the crisis of our own survival appears only to exacerbate and deepen the crisis and bring us closer to our own extinction.

We wonder how we could ever have come to this tragic impasse. After all, it's not for lack of vigilance that we find ourselves minutes away from our own elimination. Certainly, it can be said that our main pre-occupation as a species has always been to seek ways to insure our own security. How then, could a species so concerned with finding security have steered such an opposite course?

It is in the nature of a pathology for the patient to be unaware of the causes of his condition. Our pathology, our sickness is rooted in our ideas about security and the nature of what it means to be a human being. A careful diagnosis of our collective psychosis reveals the high cost we would have to pay for getting well. To cure ourselves would require a wholesale reorientation of the human psyche. To disarm the world we would first have to disarm our world view. To wage peace, we would first have to wage war against our own psyches. For it is not the bomb that is the problem. It is the kind of collective mind that could have conceived of it in the first place.

Many people believe that it is possible to extricate the bomb from the culture and still maintain the consciousness that gave rise to it. These people prefer to think of the bomb as an accident, a fluke, an indiscretion. It is none of these. We teeter on the brink of annihilation with tens of thousands of projectiles poised to seek out and destroy every vestige of life on this planet because we have chosen to do so. This is the hard reality we hide from. This is the cruel truth we seek to deny. Our nuclear policy is not an aberration. It is the logical amplification of a way of thinking that is so endemic to our way of life that we are virtually incapable of exercising any kind of independent judgement on it. For to do so would be to pass judgement on the totality of our existence from the time we first began to exercise our conscious mind; from the time we first stepped outside the gates of Paradise and stumbled forth into a world of our own making.

We talk of world cooperation, yet we teach our young that material self-interest is the motivating force of history. We talk of sharing with others but instruct our children that it is only by each individual maximizing their own selfish wants and desires that the common good is advanced. We say that life has an intrinsic value, but educate the next generation to believe that life emerged through a combination of blind chance and rank opportunism. We wonder why there is so little toleration in the world, but then inform inquiring young minds that there is only one objective reality that can be understood solely by the rational mind. We witness a world stripped of feeling, of caring, of sensibility, then acknowledge that such considerations cannot be integrated into an education system where human interactions are reduced to numbers, equations and statistics to be analyzed by computer modeling programs.

It would be easier, much easier, to blame the generals, the politicians and the war profiteers for this sad state of world affairs. But they too are but a reflection of our culture and our consciousness. If a survey were conducted, there is little doubt that the majority of their numbers would readily agree with the proposition that knowledge is power, power is control, and control is security. In this respect, they are merely the willing executioners, the servants, the handmaidens of our collective consciousness. We the species have made our intentions clear as to how we choose to approach the idea of security. The military, the politicians, the diplomats, the armament merchants are but the guarantors and protectors of our world view.

What becomes transparent in re-examining the ideas that comprise our existing world view is that it is our attitudes about "human nature" that govern the approach we take to insuring our own security. Our military stance is a reflection of the expectations we have of our fellow human beings. If, as Locke and Smith suggest, we Homo sapiens are primarily interested in maximizing our own utilitarian self-interest and material ends, then the military is right in asserting that the only way to keep the peace is to amass enough destructive weaponry to insure that the other side won't be foolish enough to try and expropriate what we have. If, as Darwin suggests, life favors those species who are the most opportunistic, then the military is right in considering a first strike strategy as a viable option. If, as Descartes suggests, the cosmos operates by precise mathematical laws, then the military experts are right in believing that they can control the totality of the world environment by reliance on sophisticated computer modeling of quantifiable data. If, as our culture contends, efficiency is the highest value of society and the measure of all things, then our war planners are right in arguing that the nuclear bomb is the best weapon ever developed. A few nuclear bombs can obliterate the entire city of New York with more fire power than was used in all of World War II by all the combatants. Certainly, from the point of view of efficiency, the nuclear bomb is faster, expropriates more and with less expenditure of time, energy and resources than any other weapon system ever devised.

The history of the nuclear arms race is the history of attempts to optimize the speed of delivery of the bomb and the amount of devastation it can do, and to minimize the time and participation necessary to do it. The military is now attempting to develop sophisticated weaponry that can travel at the speed of light, do catastrophic damage, and with no human involvement at all in the process: its employment being left up to a new generation of super computers who will think and act for us. The more efficient each generation of weapons is, the more secure the military establishment feels.

What then are we to do? Shall we continue to hold on to efficiency as the central operating method and supreme value of our society, and not adhere to it in our military planning?

Shall we continue to believe that the world can be quantified and reduced to mere statistics, numbers, equations and computer modeling, and deny its applicability in our military planning? Shall we continue to organize our economy and our society around the assumption that our species is opportunistic, greedy, self-serving and utterly utilitarian, and not apply the same standards when our political leaders map out our defense policies?

What then are we to do when the values we hold as a society, the values we pass on to our children are the same values that inextricably and inevitably lead to the conflagration of the globe?

How do we change the way we think? More appropriately, how do we change the way we think about the way we think?

The answer to this question is to be found in the posing of another question. This second question is perhaps the most important question the human family can ask itself at the present time. By the mere fact of our willingness to even consider this second question, we begin the process of changing the way we think about the way we think. To pose the question we need to establish both the context and the setting.

First the context. Think of all the benefits and potential benefits derived from splitting the atom. Now think of all the harm and potential harm derived from splitting the atom.

Next, the setting. Go back in time to December 2, 1942 at the University of Chicago. Scores of physicists were frantically at work on the top secret Manhattan Project. On that historic day, the decision had to be made as to whether or not to unleash the first sustained chain reaction. At the time, many of the scientists working on the project had reservations about going ahead. They had a glimmer of recognition of what their decision might eventually lead to. Not withstanding, the Nazi menace was beckoning at the front door. The government was looking to them for a weapon to win the war. They pulled the switch and forever changed the course of world history.

Now the question. Those scientists had only their foresight to rely on in making their decision. Now, forty years later, we have hindsight. Knowing what we know now about all of the benefits and risks associated with nuclear technology, how many of us would vote to split the atom had we to make that decision over again? How many of us would vote not to split the atom?

There can be no more troubling question. Troubling on two levels. First because we are forced to choose between accepting or rejecting the development of a technology that has both benefits and risks attached to it. Many of us would like to think that we can split our vote, saying yes to the benefits that can be derived from the technology and no to the harmful uses. Unfortunately, there is only one way to split the atom, and the knowledge gained from the experiment becomes forever part of the collective memory of the species, always available to be plucked out and used at some future time for baneful purposes.

Since all technology represents the power of expropriation, and since we have long sought power over every aspect of our environment, it seems illogical to conclude that we would ever curtail a technological revolution by circumscribing its uses only for certain kinds of control over the environment and not for others. In fact, by virtually all cases that we know of the possibilities inherent to a new technological category have been fully exploited over time, whether their purposes were benign or satanic.

Second, the issue of whether or not to split the atom raises a far more troubling set of questions. Even if the harm has exceeded the benefits, which any reasonably sane person is likely to conclude, to say no to splitting the atom seems unthinkable, maybe even as unthinkable as the decision to push the button and commit the world to nuclear annihilation. Our mind simply will not allow us to say no to the splitting of the atom, despite what we know about where that decision has led. It's as if we are compelled by some sacred pact, some higher form of allegiance we all share, to make the decision to go ahead, even against our own best judgement. Our instincts might well stir us to saying no, but the rational side, our conscious mind says we must, we have no choice, it is fated, there is no alternative, it is our burden to bear.

To say no is to condemn everything we hold dear. To reject the experiment is to threaten our world view, to question our approach to knowledge and to undermine our traditional relationship to technology. We are convinced that in saying no, we would be giving up the dream that has sustained so many generations, the dream of unfettered progress, the dream of building our own earthly Eden.

What is left unsaid, in all of the discussions about whether or not we should have split the atom, is a fear that outstrips every other. It is the fear of having to reject the way we think: the way we have conditioned our conscious mind since that first day, when we found ourselves half naked, vulnerable, exposed and alone outside the padlocked gates of Paradise. The human species has spent a million lifetimes honing its mind to seek out the knowledge of expropriation. We have used up continents and built monuments over the millennia reaching back even before there was a history to record, and in all that time, with only infrequent lapses and short respites, we have perpetually sought knowledge to obtain power to gain control to achieve our own security.

It's no wonder that so many people are convinced that the splitting of the atom was inevitable: that it represented the next stage in the evolution of human thought and that any effort to resist its realization would have been futile. They argue that the mind is always seeking new ways to control the forces of nature and exercise power over other human beings and that, consequently, splitting the atom was the logical outgrowth of the development of human consciousness.

For these people, saying no to splitting the atom is unthinkable because it would mean, above all else, giving up power. When we strip nuclear technology down to its essence, what we see, naked and exposed, is a new form of raw power, more compelling than any other ever made available to the human race. The real question raised by the splitting of the atom is the question of power. Is the extraordinary power intrinsic to the process of nuclear fission and fusion appropriate to exploit or not? This question remains poignant and undismissable whether the concern be the use of atomic power to make a bomb or to build a nuclear power plant. For, even in the latter case, where the technology is specifically designed to be beneficial to society, the question of ordinate or inordinate exercise of power must inevitably be addressed.

Like the nuclear bomb, nuclear power plants release vast

amounts of energy. While that energy is being harnessed for useful economic purposes, the power built into the process is so overwhelming as to cause fundamental dislocations in the larger ecosystem, regardless of the safeguards, regulations and controls in place.

Nuclear leaks, potential meltdowns, tons of nuclear waste that cannot be disposed of, exposure to radiation in the mining and handling of uranium, number among the most serious problems attendant on this energy technology. It is the tremendous power built into the process that creates these other problems.

In deciding whether or not to split the atom, we are really deciding on whether or not it is appropriate to harness and use the awesome power of the atom. Is the use of that form of power justifiable or not? Amory Lovins, a physicist and well-known environmentalist, says that using nuclear power to generate energy is equivalent to using a chain saw to cut butter. Still, to say no to the splitting of the atom, to reject the technology that it has spawned, is simply unimaginable. Such thoughts are at complete variance with the current state of consciousness of much of the human race.

To say no, then, to splitting the atom, is the most difficult thing the human species could ever ask of itself. Are we willing to reject the way we have acted upon the world since the dawn of Western consciousness? Are we willing to say no to the knowledge of expropriation, to give up power, to surrender control, to look for alternative ways of achieving security? Are we willing to say no, on occasion, to some of the fruits of our own technological handiwork? Are we willing to entertain the idea of radically rethinking the way we think about our relationship to each other and the planet in which we live? What price are we willing to pay for the survival of life here on earth?

Part II

The Engineered Gene

• • •

In 1945, the US dropped the first atomic bomb on Hiroshima. Several years earlier H.J. Muller had discovered that radiation from X-rays increases the mutation rate of genes. Scientists like Muller, and government officials at the Atomic Energy Commission, realized that the Atomic Age would bring with it a dramatic increase in radiation, which in turn, would have serious and harmful effects on human gene mutation. The grave concern over atomic radiation and gene mutation sparked a renewed interest in genetics research.

The Atomic Energy Commission began to pour funds into genetics research in an effort to better understand the effects of radiation on human genes. One of their grants came in the form of a pre-doctoral fellowship to a young geneticist at the University of Indiana named James Watson. He used those funds to unravel, for the first time, the molecular structure of DNA. Watson and his colleague Francis Crick won a Nobel prize for their brilliant discovery and opened up a new era in genetics research.

• • •

5
Engineering a Second Genesis

We are the only species to be blessed with the ability to reflect. Our physiology has endowed us with this rather unique attribute. We alone, of all the sentient animals, spend much of our time re-creating the past. We make history. We store memories. We honor events, people, and things long removed from the world of the senses. But it must also be acknowledged that we are quite selective in what we choose to remember. Our archives are full of memorabilia that pay tribute to our accomplishments, but devoid of any but the most brief account of the ecological costs that were exacted in the process of paving the byways of civilization.

Consider the present moment. While we continue to congratulate ourselves for the great scientific and technological strides of the modern Industrial Era, little attention is focused on the escalating environmental bill that has accompanied our journey. Yet a cursory glance at the tally should be enough to convince even the skeptic that our pretensions to progress are mercurial at best.

Civilizations are erected from the sinew of the natural endowment. In this respect, all power is ultimately extractive. We inflate ourselves always at the expense of a diminution of some portion of the biological and physical world that we live in. The point is, no civilization is built free and clear. Every civilization is indebted to the natural world from which it expropriated the resources to establish its identity and pulse. Every great society makes itself by borrowing against the future. All the great social experiments in history have been mortgaged to the hilt. And in each instance the bill has eventually come due forcing the foreclosure of the civilization.

Bear witness to the ledger for the Industrial Age. Ten generations of our kind have experienced untold material progress, making this era the most abundant single period in the long history of the human sojourn. So preoccupied have we been on tabulating up the figures on the debit side of the sheet that we have had scant time to glance at the escalating set of figures being registered on the credit side. An earth drenched in acid rain, beleaguered by chemical waste dumps and the poisoning of the oceans, lakes, rivers and aquifers. An earth fevered by the heating up of the atmosphere, and reeling in the wake of the mass extinction of nearly 17 percent of the remaining plant and animal species. An earth denuded by the loss of up to one third of the prime top soil and scarred by the extraction of nearly half of the useful metals and minerals. This too is our legacy, yet we are far more comfortable ticking off our feats than recanting our indiscretions.

The bill is coming due for the Industrial Era. For several hundred years we have been mining the burial grounds of the Carboniferous Age in search of the energy to propel the great engines of modern commerce. We have stolen our way into the long undisturbed tombs of stored sun that lie deep beneath the earth's crust, in search of coal, oil and natural gas. And now that we have exhumed much of the remains of what seemed to us to be an infinite reservoir of energy riches, we find ourselves, at last, face to face with a terrible reminder of how utterly dependent we really are on the earth's treasures for our very sustenance.

The Industrial Age has been made from fossil fuels. This simple fact begets a troubling query. Is it possible to maintain an industrial system after we run out of the materials that make it up? On the other side of this most disturbing question lies the great abyss, that no man's land where we are forced once again to begin re-imagining our civilization anew. What after the Industrial Age?

While the Industrial Age is not going to collapse in a fortnight or magically disappear in a generation or even a lifetime, its claim to the future has long since been spent. The youthful exuberance of the Industrial Era is now but a fading din. Like all great epochs, it too has begun to succumb to the ravages of time. That is not to say that the Industrial Age will not remain with us. It will, just as other great economic epochs still do. One can still travel the back waters of the planet and stumble upon faltering pockets of medieval life, or even neolithic and paleolithic life. These living museums exist as a reminder of the long continuum of human experiments over the millennia, all designed to establish an immortal kingdom inside the bowels of an all too mortal planetary womb.

Now that we are forced to move from the netherworld of stored sun back to a world bathed in sunlight, we begin a new page in our own economic travels. The world economy is making a long term transition from a non-renewable energy base to a renewable one. As fossil fuels become more scarce and the price to process, utilize and recycle them more costly, we begin to turn our attention to biological resources as the energy base of civilization.

For nearly two decades, the environmental community has championed the cause of renewable resources. In their enthusiasm, environmental leaders have somehow been led to the rather mistaken notion that the adoption of a renewable resource base for the world economy would automatically usher in a new deep ecology ethos. Indeed, environmentalists have leaped to the premature conclusion that the age of renewable resources and the age of ecology are one and the same when, in fact, they are not.

There are, in reality, two very different approaches to the Age of Biology. Of the two, the ecological alternative is likely to be the least popular and least likely to dominate.

The ecological vision is based squarely on the need to balance our budgets with nature. The guiding principle is to insure that society does not extract and consume faster than nature can reproduce. The advocates of an ecological ethos are wedded to the idea of serving as a partner rather than an overseer and exploiter of the natural environment. A premium is placed on preserving our biological and physical environment for future generations to enjoy. The prophets of an ecological vision beseech us to resacralize life at every level of existence. They ask each of us to treat all life more equitably. To live simply and in harmony with the rhythms of the ecosystem, to take only our fair share of the earth's resources, to respect the rights of all living things to fulfill their unique telos or nature. These are but a few of the central themes that animate the ecological vision of the Age of Biology.

There is another approach, however, to organizing the coming age. Genetic engineering is more than a set of products, more than a technology. It is a method for organizing the entire Age of Biology. In theory and in practice genetic engineering is so contrary to the underlying principles of the ecological vision as to constitute a totally different conception of the future.

The prime objective of genetic engineering is efficiency and speed. While genetic engineers agree with the environmentalists that a long term transformation of our resource base from non-renewables to renewables is essential and inevitable, they part company with their counterparts when it comes to the critical question of how to go about organizing the Age of Biology. To their mind, natural production and recycling schedules are woefully inadequate to ensure an accelerating standard of living for a burgeoning human population. To compensate for the tardiness of solar production, new ways must be found to engineer the genetic blueprints of microbes, plants and animals in order to accelerate their transformation into useful economic products. Engineer the genetic blueprint of a tree so that it will grow to maturity in a year. Manipulate the genetic instructions of domestic breeds to produce faster growing "super animals." Redesign the genetic information of plants to increase their rate of production. Speed and efficiency become the criteria, the means and the end of genetic engineering technology. An ever accelerating conversion of biological resources into economic utilities becomes the alpha and omega of the coming age.

Understandably, some students of history might argue that human beings have been interested in increasing production of biological resources since we first embarked on our agricultural way of life in the early Neolithic Era. That being the case, it might well be asked if genetic engineering is not simply a change in degree rather than in kind in the way we go about conceptualizing and organizing our relationship with the biological world. But while the motivation behind genetic engineering is firmly embedded in the historical consciousness of the race, the technology itself represents something qualitatively new.

Genetic engineering signals the most radical change in our relationship with the natural world since the dawn of the Age of Pyrotechnology. Up until the past decade, we were still wholly dependent on the gift of fire bestowed on us by Prometheus. Our world is forged in fire technology. Our identity is cast in the flames of the pyrotechnical arts. Fire has shaped our consciousness and our sociality. It is the defining technology of the present epoch in history.

In the 1970s, two molecular biologists accomplished a feat in the laboratory to rival the impact of fire technology. The scientists were Herbert Boyer of the University of California and Stanley Cohen of Stanford University. These men took slices of genetic material from two unrelated species and stitched them together, creating a novel new form of life on a molecular level that never existed in nature. The process is called recombinant DNA, and it revolutionizes our entire relationship to the living world.

With recombinant DNA technology it is now possible to snip, insert, stich, edit, program and produce new combinations of living things just as our ancestors were able to heat, burn, melt and solder together various inert materials creating new shapes, combinations and forms.

The transition from the Age of Pyrotechnology to the Age of Biotechnology is the most important and disturbing technological change in recorded history. To understand why this is the case, we must begin by appreciating the distinction between traditional tampering with biological organisms and genetic engineering intervention.

We have been domesticating, breeding and hybridizing animals and plants for as long as anyone cares to remember. But, in the long history of such tinkering we have been rather restrained in what we could accomplish because of the natural constraints imposed by mating walls and species borders. While nature has, on occasion, allowed us to cross natural species boundaries, it is also the case that such incursions have always been very narrowly proscribed. As Luther Burbank and a long line of his predecessors have understood, there are built-in limits to how much can be manipulated when working at the organism or species level.

Genetic engineering bypasses such restraints altogether. With this new technology, manipulation occurs not at the species level but at the genetic level. The working unit is no longer the organism, but rather the gene. The implications are enormous and far reaching.

To begin with, the entire notion of a species as a separate, recognizable entity with a unique nature or telos becomes arcane once we begin recombining genetic traits across mating walls. Two examples might best illustrate the dramatic change that genetic engineering makes in our relationship to nature.

In 1983, Harold Brinster of the University of Pennsylvania Veterinary School inserted human growth hormone genes into mice embryo. At birth, the mice expressed the human genes and grew twice as fast and twice as big as any other mice in history. These "super mice," as they were dubbed by the press, then passed the human growth hormone gene on to their offspring. A strain of mice now exists that continues to express human growth genes, generation after generation. These human genes have been permanently incorporated into the hereditary make-up of these animals.

Early in 1984, a comparable feat was accomplished in England. Scientists fused together a cell from a goat and a cell from a sheep, and placed the fertilized material into a surrogate which gave birth to a sheep-goat chimera, the first such example of the crossing of two completely unrelated species in human history.

Even with the most sophisticated form of breeding, these experiments could never be accomplished in nature. In the laboratory, however, such is no longer the case. What the public has not yet grasped is that the new genetic technologies allow us to combine genetic material across natural boundaries, turning all of life into manipulable chemical materials. This radical new form of biological manipulation changes both our concept of nature and our relationship to it. We begin to view life from the perspective of a chemist. The species or the organism no longer commands our respect or attention. Our interest now focuses increasingly on the thousands of strands of genetic information that establish the blueprints for living things.

With this new found ability to manipulate the very blueprint of living organisms, we assume a new role in the natural scheme of things. For the first time in history we become the architects of life itself. We become the creator and designer. We begin to reprogram the genetic codes of living things to suit our own cultural and economic needs. We take on the task of creating a second genesis, this time a synthetic one geared to the requisites of efficiency and productivity.

The short term benefits of this extraordinary new power are indeed seductive. Already we are being deluged by a stream of reports from the scientific community, industry and government telling of the great advances in store for society in the wake of this technological revolution. New genetically engineered cereal crops that will revolutionize agriculture and feed a hungry world. The cloning of new breeds of super animals to dramatically increase beef production. New microbes that will eat up oil spills, decompose toxic wastes, and fight natural pest enemies in the fields. Other microscopic organisms that will leach useful minerals out of metallic ore deposits, or provide new sources of cheap energy through biomass conversion. A new generation of pharmaceuticals that will provide new drugs never before dreamed of. Genetic surgery to eliminate the crippling hereditary diseases that have taken such a cruel toll on human beings over the ages. And, we are told, these first few examples only begin to scratch the surface of the great possibilities that lie ahead. With our new power to manipulate the genetic code of life, we open up a new vista of virtually unlimited possibilities. We are in the early dawn hours of a new epoch in history, one in which we become the sovereigns over our own biological destiny. Though reluctant to predict a timetable for the conversion of our species from alchemist to algenist, those involved in the biological sciences are confident that they have at last opened the door onto a new horizon, one in which the biology of the planet will be remodeled, this time in our own image. Our generation, they say, stands at the crossroads of this new journey, one whose final consequences won't be fully grasped for centuries to come.

The Biotechnical Age is being touted as a monumental leap forward for the human race. The soothsayers and scientists, the political pundits and captains of commerce are extolling the virtues of this new technological tour de force with such enthusiasm and verve, that even the doubters among us are apt to be swept up in the excitement of the moment.

At a time such as this, when all of society seems to be in the throes of a spectacular metamorphosis, we are naturally reluctant to slow the historical process by raising an eyebrow or two. It's probably fair to say that, when it comes to advancing our power and control over the forces of nature, our species has shown little willingness, of late, to temper its technological prowess by debating whether or not to proceed. Instead, we continue to indulge ourselves in the belief that if it can be done, it should be done; as if the only proper concern is to insure that no impediments are placed in the way of a successful adoption of each new increment of technological power into our daily lives.

Yet, as we have seen, if history has taught us anything it is that every new technological revolution brings with it both benefits and costs. The more powerful the technology is at expropriating and controlling the forces of nature, the more exacting the price we are forced to pay in terms of disruption and destruction wreaked on the ecosystems that sustain life. Certainly our recent experience with both the nuclear and petro-chemical revolutions bears out this most ancient truth.

It is more than a bit troubling, then, to hear our scientists, corporate leaders and politicians talk in such unqualified terms of the great marvels that await us in the coming Biotechnical Era. One can only conclude that in their zeal they are either being unmindful of the lessons of history or they are being disingenuous in their public pronouncements.

Genetic engineering represents the ultimate tool. It extends humanity's reach over the forces of nature as no other technology in history, perhaps with the one exception of the nuclear bomb, the ultimate expression of the Age of Pyrotechnology. With genetic technology we assume control over the hereditary blueprints of life itself. Can any reasonable person believe for a moment that such unprecedented power is without risk?

The question of whether we should embark on a long journey in which we become the architects of life is, along with the nuclear issue, the most important ever to face the human family. The ecological and environmental questions raised by such a prospect are mind boggling: the economic, political and ethical questions that accompany this new technology are without parallel.

We have heard much of late about the benefits of this great revolution in technology. We are long past due for a discussion of the costs. In the final analysis, we must carefully weigh both considerations in deciding whether or not we ought to embark on this particular quest, a quest that will intimately effect all future generations of life on this planet.

6
Creating the Efficient Gene

The great underlying myth of the Biotechnical Revolution is that it is possible to accelerate the production of more efficient living utilities without ever running out. This grand illusion will not be easy to dismiss or shunt aside. It has gained widespread currency over the past few decades because of the unfortunate choice of words we have come to use in distinguishing between fossil fuels and biological resources. We often refer to the former as non-renewable and to the later as renewable. Therein lies the nub of the problem. In actuality, living resources are as depletable and finite as fossil fuels. Somewhere down the road, however, we have managed to confuse the idea of reproducible resources with the idea of perpetually inexhaustible resources. They are not the same. Living resources reproduce, but the life support systems that nourish them do not.

The genetic engineers refuse to come to grips with this underlying reality. Instead they continue to talk of the ever accelerating production of living things firmly convinced that the information coded in the genetic instructions provides the key to unlimited output. To illustrate this point, consider the possibility of genetically engineering new plants that could absorb greater sunlight and increase the rate of photosynthesis. While the benefit of such a procedure seems apparent, at first glance, a closer examination reveals the price that would have to be paid to achieve the desired results.

Increased photosynthesis would require a greater use of soil nutrients, thus threatening the further depletion and erosion of an already endangered agricultural soil base. Soil depletion and erosion is one of the major problems in agriculture today. Up to one-third of some of our prime agricultural top-soil has been depleted in the past three decades, largely as a result of the accelerated production tempo of green revolution farming. Attempts to genetically engineer increases in speed of maturation and gross productivity will place additional burdens on an already over-taxed soil structure, thus posing the very real danger of inadequate nutrient reserves for sustaining future agricultural crops.

Genetic engineering will unquestionably result in the short term acceleration of biological materials into useful economic products, but at the expense of depleting the reservoir of life-support materials that are essential for maintaining the reproductive viability of living organisms in the future. In nature, there is no such thing as a free lunch. All biological and physical phenomena are subject to entropy and the Second Law of Thermodynamics. Being able to store and program the genetic instructions for living things is of little help if the biotic environment is bereft of the nutrients to sustain life.

All great technological revolutions secure the present by mortgaging the future. In this respect, genetic engineering represents the ultimate lien on the future. Genetic engineering raises the interest rates that will have to be paid by future generations beyond anything we've ever experienced in the long history of our attempts to control the forces of nature.

Everytime we choose to introduce a new genetically modified organism into the environment the ecological interest rate moves up a point. That's because every genetically engineered product presents a potential threat to the ecosystem it is released in. To appreciate why this is so, we need to be able to understand some of the defining characteristics of engineered organisms. The best way to do that is to contrast biotechnical products with petro-chemical products.

Genetically engineered products differ from petro-chemical products in several important ways. Because they are alive, genetically engineered products are inherently more unpredictable than petro-chemicals in the way they interact with other living things in the environment. Consequently, it is much more difficult to assess all of the potential impacts that a biotechnical product might have on the earth's ecosystems.

Genetically engineered products also reproduce. They grow and they migrate. Unlike petro-chemical products, it is impossible to constrain them within a given geographical locale. Finally, once released, it is virtually impossible to recall living products back to the laboratory, especially those products that are microscopic in nature. For all these reasons, genetically engineered products pose far greater long-term potential risks to the environment than petro-chemical substances.

Exactly how dangerous are genetically engineered products? Environmental scientists tell us that the risks in releasing biotechnical products into the biosphere are comparable to those we've encountered in introducing exotic organisms into the North American habitat. Over the past several hundred years thousands of non-native organisms have been brought to America from other regions of the globe. While most of these creatures have adapted to the ecosystem without severe dislocations, a small percentage of them have run wild, wreaking havoc on the flora and fauna of the continent. Gypsy moth, Kudzu vine, Dutch elm disease, chestnut blight, starlings, Mediterranean fruit flies come easily to mind. Each year the American continent is ravaged by these non-native organisms, with destruction to plant and animal life running into the tens of billions of dollars.

Whenever a genetically engineered organism is released there is always a small chance that it too will run amok because, like exotic organisms, it is not a naturally occurring life form. It has been artificially introduced into a complex environment that has developed a web of highly synchronized relationships over millions of years. Each new synthetic introduction is tantamount to playing ecological roulette. That is, while there is only a small chance of it triggering an environmental explosion, if it does, the consequences can be thunderous and irreversible.

For example, consider the first set of experiments in the US to release a genetically engineered organism into the open environment. Researchers at the University of California have modified a bacteria called P-syringae. This particular bacteria is found in its naturally occurring state in temperate regions all over the world. Its most unique attribute is its ability to nucleate ice crystals. In other words, it helps facilitate the formation of frost or ice. Using recombinant DNA technology, University of California researchers have found a way to delete the genetic instructions for making ice from the bacteria. This new genetically modified P-syringae microbe is called ice-minus.

Scientists are excited about the long-term commercial possibilities of ice-minus in agriculture. Frost damage has long been a major problem for American farmers. The chief culprit has been P-syringae which attaches itself to the plants, creating ice crystals. The American corporation financing this research hopes that by spraying massive concentrations of ice-minus P-syringae on agricultural crops, the naturally occurring P-syringae will be edged out, providing a protective blanket against frost damage. The benefits in introducing this genetically engineered organism appear impressive. It's only when one looks at the long-term ecological costs that problems begin to surface.

To begin with, the first question a good environmental scientist would ask is what role does the naturally occurring P-syringae play in nature? The experts that have studied this particular organism say that its ice-making capacity helps shape worldwide precipitation patterns and is a key determinant in establishing climatic conditions on the planet. The experts also contend that the P-syringae bacteria has played an important evolutionary role in enhancing the viability of frost resistant plants and insects in the northern areas of the globe.

Many of our agricultural crops, however, are tropical in origin and frost sensitive like citrus, corn, beans and tomatoes. Now consider the prospect of spraying ice-minus bacteria on millions of acres of frost-sensitive crops over several decades. While the crops will be protected against frost, the local flora and fauna will be at a disadvantage as the naturally occurring ice-nucleating bacteria which they have relied on for millions of years will have been edged out. Blanketing millions of acres of agricultural land with ice-minus also provides a protective coat of warmth allowing tropical based insects to begin migrating into colder regions. Then too, what will be the long-term effect on worldwide precipitation patterns and climate if ice-minus replaces the ice-making bacteria over millions of acres of land for a sustained period of time?

Introducing just this one genetically engineered product into the environment raises disturbing ecological questions. Yet, in the coming decades, industry is expected to introduce thousands of new genetically engineered products into the environment each year, just as industry introduced thousands of petro-chemical products into the environment each year. While many of these genetically engineered organisms will prove to be benign, sheer statistical probability suggests that a small percentage will prove to be dangerous and highly destructive to the environment.

For example, scientists are considering the possibility of producing a genetically engineered enzyme that could destroy lignin, an organic substance that makes wood rigid. They believe there might be great commercial advantage in using this genetically modified organism to clean up the effluent from paper mills or for decomposing biological material for energy. But if the enzyme were to migrate offsite and spread through forest land, it could well end up destroying millions of acres of woodland by eating away at the substance that provides trees with their rigidity.

Several years ago, General Electric developed and patented a micro-organism that eats up oil spills. This new microscopic creation has never been let out, probably for the reason that there is no way to guarantee that it won't get loose, reproduce in mass volumes and begin eating up oil reserves in gasoline storage tanks all over the planet. Environmental scientists also warn that new micro-organisms designed to consume toxic materials might develop an appetite for more valuable resources.

In fact, the long-term cumulative impact of thousands upon thousands of introductions of genetically modified organisms could well eclipse by a magnitude the damage that has resulted from the wholesale release of petro-chemical products into the earth's ecosystems. With these new biological based products, however, the damage is not containable, the destructive effects continue to reproduce, and the organisms can not be recalled, making the process irreversible.

Many people labor under the misguided assumption that genetic engineering has a good side and a bad side, and that steps can be taken to regulate potential abuses, assuring that only the beneficial aspects of the technology are employed. They fail to understand that it is the built-in assumptions of the technology, the inherent logic of the process, that creates the problem regardless of the good or bad intention of those using it. This can be seen quite clearly when looking at genetic engineering in agriculture and animal husbandry. The objective of genetic engineering technology is to improve the efficiency and productive output of plants and domestic animals. Efficiency and productivity, however, are cultural values not ecological rules.

Engineering efficiency and productivity into plants and animals means engineering sustainability out. Every breeder knows that attempts to streamline the productive efficiency of plants and animals results in more lucrative but less fit strains and breeds. It has long been acknowledged that over-breeding and over-hybridization result in monoculturing and loss of genetic variability. Reliance on a few super strains or breeds has proven to be very unwise, because it increases vulnerability to specific diseases or radical changes in the environment. Genetic diversity assures that each species will have enough variety to effectively adapt to changing environments. By eliminating all of the so called unprofitable strains and breeds, we undermine the adaptive capacity of each species. Farmers have witnessed, first hand, the problem that can arise from monoculturing. Not long ago the corn farmers were hit with a devastating blight. The corn strain they were all using was particularly vulnerable to the disease, resulting in massive losses. Had they planted a variety of corns, some of the strains would have been hearty enough to ward off the pest.

Animal breeding has posed similar problems. For example, many dairy farmers have chosen to breed only Holsteins because of their superior milk yield. Other less lucrative breeds have all but disappeared. The Holstein, while more lucrative, is less fit. It relies on specialized feeds, an array of technological support systems and continual monitoring, and cannot survive in pasture land over winter like other breeds.

Genetic engineering technology will dramatically accelerate

the problems of monoculturing and loss of gene diversity. This technology allows scientists to more effectively increase short-term productivity by engineering efficiency directly into the genetic code of a species. At the same time, non-useful traits can be deleted directly from the hereditary blueprint further to increase productive output. There is even talk about introducing cloning techniques on a large scale in agriculture and animal husbandry over the next several decades. By reproducing millions of identical copies of a single superior strain or breed, agriculturists hope to increase efficiency and output dramatically. This kind of pure monoculturing is going to result in the almost complete loss of minor strains or breeds, as they will be considered uneconomical and uncompetitive in the open marketplace. The long-term environmental consequences could be profound. Imagine millions of exact cloned replicas of a particular cow being used throughout the country and the world. The spread of one disease to which that particular genotype is not immune could result in the wholesale destruction of entire herds and the collapse of much of the dairy industry. It could take years to search for any remaining minor breeds as replacements, and decades more to rebreed new herds from them.

Cloning livestock only begins to touch on the possibilities that lie ahead. Even more ambitious are current experiments being conducted by the US Department of Agriculture to insert human growth hormone genes into the permanent hereditary make-up of pigs, sheep and other domestic animals. Some scientists predict that within a very few years barnyard animals will double in size and develop to maturity in half the normal time. It is possible, say the experts, that with genetic engineering technology, they could produce a cow the size of a small elephant, producing over 45,000 pounds of milk products per year.

By transferring genes from one species into the biological codes of another species it is possible to change the essential character of domestic animals. These changes will not only revolutionize the business of animal husbandry, but also our concept of nature as well. As already mentioned, in accepting the notion of transferring genes from one species into another, we begin the process of eliminating species' borders from our thinking. Already researchers in the field of molecular biology are arguing that there is nothing particularly sacred about the concept of a species. As they see it, the important unit of life is no longer the organism, but rather the gene. They increasingly view life from the vantage point of the chemical composition at the genetic level. From this reductionist perspective, life is merely the aggregate representation of the chemicals that give rise to it and therefore they see no ethical problem whatsoever in transferring one, five or a hundred genes from one species into the hereditary blueprint of another species. For they truly believe that they are only transferring chemicals coded in the genes and not anything unique to a specific animal. By this kind of reasoning, all of life becomes desacralized. All of life becomes reduced to a chemical level and becomes available for manipulation.

Some ethicists and professional observers of science say they are not concerned about these first few experiments, but would be concerned with the transfer of more sophisticated genetic traits. Unfortunately, they fail to see that the blurring of species' borders begins the first moment a human gene is permanently implanted into the hereditary make-up of a mouse, pig or sheep. It is the first experiment that legitimizes the process. After all, if there is nothing particularly sacred about the human growth hormone gene, as researchers contend, then they might just as well argue that there is nothing particularly unique or special about all of the thousands of other individual genes that make-up the human gene pool. When it comes to more complex human traits (polygenic) that influence behavior and intellectual capacity, researchers will undoubtedly argue that they are not unique either, since they are merely a composite of the chemicals coded in the individual genes that make them up.

What, then, is unique about the human gene pool, or any other mammalian gene pool? Nothing, if you view each species as merely the sum total of the chemicals coded in the individual genes that make it up. It is this radical new concept of life that legitimizes the idea of crossing all species' barriers, and undermines the inviolability of discrete, recognizable species in nature.

Many scientists contend that it would be wrong to discontinue these kinds of experiments, because they broaden our field of knowledge. They rely on the rather clichéd argument that to halt such research would constitute a form of censorship. This is nonsense. Just because something can be done is no longer adequate justification for arguing that it should be done. The point is, it is a bit foolish to argue that every scientific experiment is worth pursuing. If certain types of scientific activity undermine the ethical principles and canons of civilization, we have an obligation to ourselves and future generations to be willing to say no. That doesn't make us guilty of stifling freedom of inquiry or "progress." It simply makes us responsible human beings.

Other proponents of this research argue that species have evolved, one from the other over the long period of history and, as such, the process of genetic transfer is merely a speed up of evolutionary development. On the other hand, it is also true that since Homo sapiens have populated the earth, we have never once recorded an event where one species has mutated into another species. Even accepting that these occurrences have taken place before human eyes could have ever recorded the events, we know little or nothing about how or why such changes might have occurred. In contrast, with the new genetic technologies we have the tools to "evolve" our own concept of life in a dramatically short span of historical time. Should we allow the cultural biases of a particular moment in human history to dictate basic changes in the biological blueprint of animals and humans? Should social criteria like efficiency, profits, productivity and national security determine which traits should be transferred between species? These are profound questions deserving long and prudent public debate. The time to discuss these questions is before the process unfolds, not after the technology has run its course.

7
A New Form of Imperialism

The problem of loss of gene diversity and monoculturing has led to a new international crisis of overwhelming proportions. Seed varieties and animal breeds which used to be plentiful are now becoming rare resources. The giant multinational corporations are scouting the four corners of the planet in search of wild strains of plants and rare breeds of animals whose genetic characteristics might be useful in the development of a new generation of agricultural crops, domesticated herds, pharmaceuticals and other products.

As we make the long-term transition from the Industrial Age to the Biotechnical Age, the world's germ plasm will become as important to the economic fortunes of each country as fossil fuels and metals were during the brief expanse of the Industrial Era. Germplasm is the fundamental resource of the Genetic Age, and because the worldwide supply of wild strains of seeds and breeds of animals is dwindling fast, the developed nations and the transnational corporations are engaged in a concerted drive to gain control over this precious reservoir of biological treasure. Their efforts have already led to a wholesale transfer of rare germplasm from southern-hemisphere countries, where most of the remaining varieties exist, to northern countries where the genetic engineering revolution is based. Today over 92 percent of the world's stored germplasm is already controlled in specially designed gene banks that have been established within the national borders of the key biotechnical powers. The industrial nations are asserting a new form of international imperialism, this time over the genetic pool of the planet. Control over raw genetic resources will ensure control of the Genetic Age.

Third world nations are beginning to mobilize in opposition to what they perceive as a new and insidious form of colonialism. In various United Nations forums over the past decade, third world countries have argued that the biotechnical powers are robbing them of their national heritage and, in so doing, forcing them into a new form of servitude. With control over genetic resources, genetic technologies and worldwide marketing and distribution of genetic products, the transnational corporations and their host nations will be able to successfully exploit the southern hemisphere countries during the coming Biotechnical Age just as they did during the Industrial Age, when they controlled much of the world's nonrenewable resources, industrial technologies and distribution of petro-chemical products.

A new form of international politics is emerging with the transition into the Biotechnical Age. In the decades to come, southern countries and northern countries are going to lock horns in a fierce and protracted battle over control of the genetic pool of the planet.

8
The Gene Gap

Genetic engineering is the most powerful technology we have ever conceived to control the forces of nature. Is it any wonder, then, that governments all over the world are beginning to assess the military potential of this new tool? In 1984, the *Wall Street Journal* ran an unprecedented seven part series on its editorial page warning that the Soviet leadership had embarked on an ambitious program to develop a new generation of biological weapons to equal the potential destructive power of nuclear weaponry.

The US military is also becoming increasingly interested in the use of recombinant DNA technology. According to the National Science Foundation, expenditures on all biological research by the Department of Defense increased by 59 percent between 1980 and the end of 1983. The Pentagon contends that its interest is purely defensive and that its main preoccupation is on developing useful vaccines that could ward off an enemy attack.

Military spokesmen point out that the US, the Soviet Union and many other nations are signatories of the 1972 Biological Weapons Convention, which bans the development and stockpiling of biological weapons for offensive purposes. That treaty, however, does allow for the development of certain biological agents for defensive purposes, like vaccines.

Under the guise of vaccine development, the US and the USSR are experimenting with every super pathogen known to humanity, from diphtheria and Rift Valley fever to legionnaire's disease and anthrax.

These deadly viruses can be easily recombined with normal

bacteria like E. coli and mass produced in quantities that could destroy every living thing on earth. It is also possible to use recombinant DNA techniques in guerrilla warfare. Scientists say they may be able to clone selective toxins to eliminate specific racial or ethnic groups whose genotypical make-up predisposes them to certain disease patterns. Genetic engineering can also be used to destroy specific strains of agricultural plants or domestic animals if the intent is to cripple a particular national economy.

While both governments claim that their work is only defensive in nature, it is widely acknowledged that it is virtually impossible to distinguish between defensive and offensive research in this field. Writing in the November 1983 edition of the *Bulletin of Atomic Scientists*, Robert J. Sinzheimer, a renowned biophysicist, and chancellor of the University of California at Santa Cruz, observed that, because of the nature of this particular category of experimentation, there is no adequate way to properly distinguish between peaceful uses of deadly toxins and military uses. According to Sinzheimer, experiments like the kind being considered today could be used to advance the knowledge of how to develop biological weapons as well.

The Stockholm International Peace Research Institute's exhaustive study on chemical and biological warfare concurs with Sinzheimer's assessment, concluding that "some common forms of vaccine production are very close technically to production of CBW agents and so offer easy opportunities for conversion."

Dr. Richard Goldstein, professor of microbiology of Harvard Medical School, sums up the nature of these kinds of biological experiments currently being conducted by the DOD. Under the banner of defensive purposes, the DOD "can justify working with the super pathogens of the world – producing altered and more virulent strains, producing vaccines for protection of their troops against such agents . . . and likewise for the development of dispersal systems since DOD must be able to defend against any such dispersal system. Under this guise, what DOD ends up with is a new biological weapon system – a virulent organism, a vaccine against it, and a dispersal system. As you can gather from this, there is but a very thin line – if any – between such a defensive system (allowed by the convention) and any prohibited offensive system."

We have known for several years now that recombinant DNA technology is a powerful tool: one that could be used for mass destructive purposes. As far back as 1976, the Federation of American Scientists Public Interest Report stated:

> *Few doubt that this technology has the potential for deliberate misuse to produce great dangers. Genes from disease-causing (pathogenic) organisms, or from organisms that produce highly toxic agents, could be implanted in hosts capable of rapid spread, so as to produce dramatic new biological dangers . . . The world must begin to face a biological proliferation threat that might, before long, rival that of nuclear weapons.*

A new type of arms race looms ominously on the horizon. The super powers are beginning to whisper out loud about the "gene gap" in terms reminiscent of the paranoia that gave rise to the "missile gap" rhetoric of the 1960s. Professional military observers are not sanguine about the prospect of keeping the genetics revolution out of the hands of the war planners. As a tool of mass destruction, it rivals nuclear weaponry, and it can be developed at a fraction of the cost. These two factors alone make genetic technology an ideal weapon of the future.

Our own Department of Defense has already made clear its intentions not to fall behind the Soviets in genetic engineering technology. In the Fall of 1984, the Defense Department requested and received from Congress authorization to begin construction of a new biological warfare test laboratory at Dugway Proving Grounds in the Utah desert. At the time of the authorization, Defense Secretary Caspar Weinberger told members of Congress that he had obtained "new evidence that the Soviet Union has maintained its offensive biological warfare program and that it is exploring genetic engineering to expand its program's scope." Weinberger went on to warn the Congress that "it is essential and urgent that we develop and field adequate biological and toxin protection."

While the new biological warfare laboratory at Dugway is being categorized as a defensive test facility, the military has acknowledged that it will be experimenting with "substantial volumes" of some of the most hazardous biological agents known to exist. It is a certainty that the Soviet Union will perceive this latest development as a direct threat to its own national security and will respond in kind with a further escalation of its own so-called "defensive program," thus hastening the emergence of a new and deadly arms race with genetic engineering technology.

In this century, modern science reached its apex with the splitting of the atom, followed in close pursuit by the splitting of the DNA nucleus. The first discovery led immediately to the development of the atomic bomb, leaving humanity to ponder, for the first time in history, the prospect of an end to its own future on earth. Can any of us doubt for a moment that the other great scientific breakthrough of our time will soon be used in a comparable manner, posing a similar threat to our very existence as a species?

9

Genetic Politics

Any thoughtful probe of genetic engineering technology must eventually wind its way toward a discussion of eugenics. Genetic engineering technology and eugenics are inseparably linked. To grapple with one requires a willingness to wrestle with the other.

The term eugenics was conceived by Sir Francis Galton in the nineteenth century and is generally dichotomized in the following way. Negative eugenics involves the systematic elimination of so-called biologically undesirable traits. Positive eugenics is concerned with the use of genetic manipulation to "improve" the characteristics of an organism or species.

As a social philosophy, eugenics found its first real home here in America at the turn of the century. The rediscovery of Mendel's laws spurred renewed interest in heredity within the scientific community which, in turn, ignited a eugenics flame in the popular culture. Before that flame was finally extinguished during the Great Depression, American culture was fully saturated with eugenics dogma. Public opinion came to express the belief that blood ties and heredity were far more important in shaping individual behavior and in determining the status of various ethnic and social groups than economic, social or cultural determinants. Many Americans preferred to place their trust in nature over nurture and the quickened eugenics sentiment of the time steamrollered its way into public policy, blackening the American spirit for a brief historical moment.

Before running its course, the early eugenics movement imprinted its image directly on state and federal laws. Many states adopted sterilization statutes, and the US Congress passed a new immigration law in the 1920s based on eugenics doctrine. In the years that followed, thousands of American citizens were sterilized so they could not pass on their "inferior" traits, and the Federal Government locked its doors to certain immigrant groups deemed biologically unfit by then-existing eugenics standards.

The American experience with eugenics was soon dwarfed by the eugenics campaign initiated by the Third Reich. Determined to rid the world of all but the "pure" Aryan race, Adolf Hitler orchestrated a campaign of terror and mass genocide of such overwhelming magnitude that it is likely to remain the darkest shadow ever cast over the human experience. Over six million Jews and members of other religious and ethnic groups were rounded up from all over the European continent and interned in giant concentration camps. Convinced that these human beings were biologically unfit, the Third Reich committed itself to expunging their genetic inheritance from the human gene pool. The high command called it the final solution – the systematic elimination of an entire people by gassing in crematoria all over the continent.

At the same time, the Nazis launched an ambitious positive eugenics campaign, in which carefully screened Aryan women were selected to mate with elite SS officers. The pregnant women were housed and cared for in specially designated state facilities, and their offspring were offered up to the Third Reich as the representatives of the new super race that would rule the world for the next millennium.

After World War II, many voiced the hope that eugenics had finally come to rest alongside the mass unmarked graves that scarred the European landscape. Their hopes were to be shortlived. Beginning early in the 1970s the world began to hear scattered reports of great scientific breakthroughs occurring in the new field of molecular biology. By the mid 1980s those reports have cascaded into a torrent of new discoveries, so astonishing in scope that a somewhat bewildered public is finding itself unprepared to assess the full social implications. Of one thing, however, the public is fast becoming aware. Our scientists are developing the most powerful set of tools for manipulating the biological world ever conceived. This newfound power over the life force of the planet is raising once again the spectre of a new eugenics movement. After all, eugenics is defined as the systematic effort to manipulate the genetic inheritance of an organism or group of organisms to create a more "perfect" species. Now our scientists are providing us with tools that are, by their very nature, eugenic. This is the terrible reality that so few policy makers are willing to grasp.

The new genetic engineering tools are designed to be eugenics instruments. Whenever recombinant DNA, cell fusion and other related genetic techniques are used to improve the genetic blueprints of a microbe, plant, animal or human being, a eugenics consideration is built into the process itself.

Much of genetic engineering is concerned with changing the genetic characteristics of a species. In laboratories all across the globe, molecular biologists are making daily decisions about what genes to alter, insert and delete from the hereditary code of an organism. These are eugenic decisions. Every time a genetic change of this kind is made, the scientist, the corporation or the state is tacitly, if not explicitly, making decisions about what are the good genes that should be inserted and preserved and what are the bad genes that should be altered or deleted. This is exactly what eugenics is all about. Genetic engineering is a technology designed to enhance the genetic inheritance of living things by manipulating their genetic code.

Some might take offense at the idea that eugenics is built into the new genetic engineering technology. They prefer to equate eugenics with the Nazi experience of four decades ago. The new eugenics movement, however, bears no resemblance to the reign of terror that culminated with the holocaust. The US and the world is unlikely to witness the emergence of a new social eugenics movement in the foreseeable future. It is more likely that we will see the emergence of a wholly new kind of eugenics movement, one in which there are no evil conspirators, no faustian figures, no machiavellian institutions which we could conveniently point to as instigators and purveyers. The new eugenics is commercial eugenics, not social eugenics. The evil, if there is any, is the human compulsion for a better way of life, for a brighter, more promising future for succeeding generations.

Is it wrong to want healthier babies? Is it wrong to want more efficient food crops and livestock and improved sources of energy? Is it wrong to seek new ways to improve our standard of living? Genetic engineering is coming to us not as a sinister plot, but rather as a social and economic boon. Still, we ought not to confuse the good intentions of the creators of this science with the logic of the technology. Try as we will, there is simply no way to get around the fact that every decision that is made to alter the hereditary make-up of an organism or a species is a eugenics decision.

In the decades and centuries to come scientists will learn more about how the genes function. They will learn how to map more of the individual genetic traits and they will become increasingly adept at turning the genes on and off. They will become more sophisticated in the techniques of recombining genes and altering genetic codes. At every step of the way conscious decisions will have to be made as to which kind of permanent changes in the biological codes of life are worth pursuing and which are not. A society and civilization steeped in "engineering" the gene pool of the planet cannot possibly hope to escape the kind of ongoing eugenics decisions that go hand in hand with each new technological foray.

There will be enormous social pressure to conform with the underlying logic of genetic engineering, especially when it comes to its human applications. Every prospective parent will be forced to decide whether to take their chances with the traditional genetic lottery or program specific traits in or out of their baby at conception. If they choose to go with the traditional approach, letting genetic fate determine their child's biological destiny, they could find themselves in deep trouble if something goes dreadfully wrong from a genetic perspective: something they could have avoided had they availed themselves of corrective genetic intervention at the embryo stage.

Consider the following scenario. Two parents decide not to program their fetus. The child is born with a deadly genetic disease. The child dies prematurely and needlessly. The genetic trait responsible for the disease could have been deleted from the fertilized egg by simple gene surgery. In the

Genetic Age, a parent's failure to intervene with corrective genetic engineering of the embryo might well be regarded as a heinous crime. Society will undoubtedly conclude that every parent has a responsibility to provide as safe and secure an environment as humanly possible for their unborn child. Not to do so would be considered a breech of parental duty for which the parents would be morally if not legally culpable.

With the introduction of an array of new human reproduction technologies, the choices become even more problematic. In the coming decades molecular biologists will map the specific genes for hundreds of monogenic disorders, providing prospective parents with a complete and accurate listing of the specific genetic defects they will likely pass on to their offspring. In the past, a parent's genetic history provided markers for speculation, but there was still no way to know for sure whether specific genetic traits would be passed on. In the future, the guesswork will be increasingly eliminated posing a moral dilemma for prospective parents. Parents will have at their disposal a more and more accurate readout of their individual genetic make-ups, and will be able to predict the statistical probability of specific genetic disorders being passed on to their children as a result of their biological union.

At that point, parents will have to make critical choices. Whether to go ahead using their own egg and sperm, knowing their children will inherit certain "undesirable" traits, or whether to substitute either egg or sperm with a donor through in vitro fertilization, embryo transfers and other emerging human reproduction techniques.

While ethicists contend that these artificial reproduction procedures have, at best, only a limited market, they ignore the commercial compulsion to expand and create a universal marketplace for new technologies. Prospective parents will be cautioned that if they have any significant risk factor in their genetic make-up that might adversely effect their offspring, they would be better off purchasing either untainted sperm or healthier eggs rather than relying on their own biological assets.

The new human reproduction technologies are likely to be as aggressively marketed as baby formula was over the past two decades. Only a small percentage of women really needed the artificial milk for nursing, yet the multi-national corporations convinced millions of women all over the world to switch from natural breast feeding to their synthetic process, under the guise that the artificial substitute was cleaner, healthier, more scientific and progressive. There is every reason to expect a similar corporate approach to selling the new human reproduction procedures.

Advocates of human genetic engineering argue that it would be irresponsible not to use this new tool to help prevent deadly, disabling and disfiguring diseases. What they apparently overlook is the fact that there are at least 2,000 monogenic diseases alone. Should they all be eliminated from the hereditary code of our species over the coming centuries? Does it makes sense to monoculture the human germ line as we have with domestic plants and animals, eliminating recessive traits that our species might need in the future to adapt to changing environmental conditions?

Once we decide to begin the process of human genetic engineering, there is really no logical place to stop. If diabetes, sickle cell anemia, and cancer are to be cured by altering the genetic make-up of an individual, why not proceed to other "disorders": myopia, color blindness, left-handedness? Indeed, what is to preclude a society from deciding that a certain skin color is a disorder? In fact, why would we ever say no to any alteration of the genetic code that might enhance the well-being of the individual or the species? It would be difficult to even imagine society rejecting any genetic modification that promised to improve, in some way, the performance of the human race.

The idea of engineering the human species is very similar to the idea of engineering a piece of machinery. An engineer is constantly in search of new ways to improve the performance of a machine. As soon as one set of imperfections is eliminated, the engineer immediately turns his attention to the next set of imperfections, always with the idea in mind of creating a perfect piece of machinery. Engineering is a process of continual improvement in the performance of a machine, and the idea of setting arbitrary limits to how much "improvement" is acceptable is alien to the entire engineering conception.

Whenever we begin to discuss the idea of genetic defects,

there is no way to limit the discussion to one or two or even a dozen so-called disorders, because of a hidden assumption that lies behind the very notion of "defective." Ethicist Daniel Callahan penetrates to the core of the problem when he observes that "behind the human horror at genetic defectiveness lurks . . . an image of the perfect human being. The very language of 'defect,' 'abnormality,' 'disease,' and 'risk,' presupposes such an image, a kind of proto-type of perfection."

The question, then, is whether or not humanity should begin the process of engineering future generations of human beings by technological design in the laboratory. What is the price we pay for embarking on a course whose final goal is the "perfection" of the human species? How important is it that we eliminate all the imperfections, all the defects? What price are we willing to pay to extend our lives, to ensure our own health, to do away with all the inconveniences, the irritations, the nuisances, the infirmities, the suffering, that are so much a part of the human experience? Are we so enamored with the idea of physical perpetuation at all costs that we are even willing to subject the human species to rigid architectural design?

With human genetic engineering, we get something and we give up something. In return for securing our own physical well-being we are forced to accept the idea of reducing the human species to a technologically designed product. Genetic engineering poses the most fundamental of questions. Is guaranteeing our health worth trading away our humanity?

Throughout history some people have always controlled the futures of other people. The politics of the biotechnical age are no exception. Every new biotechnical discovery will affect the power that some people exercise over others. The exercise of political power in the coming age will raise terrifying questions. For example, whom would we trust with the decision of what is a good gene that should be added to the gene pool and what is a bad gene that should be eliminated? Would we trust the federal government? The corporations? The university scientists? A group of our peers? From this perspective, few of us are able to point to any institution or group of individuals we would entrust with decisions of such import. However, if, instead of the above question, we were asked whether we would sanction new bioengineering products that could provide new sources of food and energy and enhance the physical and mental well-being of people, we would not hesitate for a moment to add our support. Yet all biologically engineered products require that someone make a decision about which genes should be engineered and which genes should be done away with. How, then, is it possible for people to be leery of trusting anyone with authority over genetic technology and at the same time be in favor of the development of the technology itself?

The answer is to be found in the nature of the question. The first question deals with power in a vacuum. No one is willing blindly to hand power over his own future to someone else – especially when it involves the engineering of life itself. The second question, however, deals with the exchange of power for material security. Virtually everyone is willing to give up some of his own power in return for being guaranteed a measure of material security in return. Exchanging power for security is the nature of politics.

The population at large has already made its intentions clear, so far as the politics of the Biotechnical Age are concerned. An unwritten contract of sorts has already been agreed upon, and without the wrangling and negotiations that usually accompany the struggle over exchange of power. The power to control the future biological design of living tissue has been signed over to the scientists, the corporations and the state without ceremony. In return, all that is being asked for are useful products that will enhance human survival and provide for the general well-being.

At first blush, the bargain appears a good one. Biotechnology has much to offer. But, as with other organizing modes throughout history, the final costs have not yet been calculated. Granting power to a specific institution or group of individuals to determine a better-engineered crop or animal or a new human hormone seems such a trifle in comparison with the potential returns. It is only when one considers the lifetime of the agreement that the full import of the politics of the Biotechnical Age becomes apparent.

Power is the exercise of control over the future. Throughout history humanity has been gradually increasing its power by extending its control over broader temporal horizons. Over the coming centuries, the ultimate exercise of power will come well within our grasp: the ability to control the future of all living things by engineering their entire life process in advance, making them a hostage of their own architecturally designed blueprints. Bioengineering represents the power of authorship. Never before in history has such complete power over life been a possibility. The idea of imprisoning the entire life cycle of an organism by simply engineering its organizational blueprint at conception is truly awesome.

In these early stages of the Age of Biotechnology such power, though formidable, appears so far removed from any potential threat to the human physiology as to be of little concern. We are more than willing to allow the rest of the living kingdom to fall under the shadow of the engineering scalpel, as long as it produces some concrete utilitarian benefit for us. We are even willing to subject parts of our anatomy to bioengineering, if it will enhance our physical and mental health. The problem is that biotechnology has a beginning but no end. Cell by cell, tissue by tissue, organ by organ, we give up our bodies as we give up our political power, a piece at a time. In the process, each loss is compensated for with a perceived gain until there is nothing more to exchange. It is at that very point that the cost of our agreement becomes visible. But it is also exactly at that point that we no longer possess the very thing we were so anxious to preserve: our own security. In the decades and centuries to come, we humans will barter ourselves away, a piece at a time, in exchange for some measure of temporary well-being. In the end, the security we fought so hard to preserve will have disappeared forever. Thanks to bioengineering, we will finally have been extricated from the great burden of human history, the unremittent need to anticipate and secure our own future. Security will no longer be our concern, because we will no longer control any measure of our own destiny. Our future will be determined at conception. It will be programmed into our biological blueprint.

Already, the breathtaking advances in genetic engineering

are being followed in close pursuit by the emergence of a new sociology; one tailored to the political prerequisites of a biotechnically controlled society. Sociobiology has emerged from the academic corridors of Harvard University and other elite educational institutions to become the sociological wing of the genetic age. In the age-old battle of nature vs nurture, the sociobiologists side with the former school of thought, arguing that human behavior is more closely associated with one's biological inheritance. While the sociobiologists acknowledge that environment can play a role in individual and group development, they are far more impressed with the role that the genes play in determining one's sociality. The political implications of this new sociobiological interpretation of human behavior are likely to be profound in the decades to come.

It is important to remember that for most of this century, the social scientists argued that it is only by affecting changes in the environment that the evils of the social order could be purged and the journey to an earthly cornucopia be assured. The orthodox political wisdom has long favored nurture over nature. Now, plagued by deepening social crises, the industrial nations seem no longer able to affect fundamental changes by the traditional path of institutional and environmental reform. The sociobiologists and others of their ilk contend that attempting to overhaul the economic and social system is at best a palliative, and at worst a useless exercise in futility. The key to all social and economic behavior, they contend, is to be found at the genetic level. To change society, they claim, we must first be willing to change the genes, for they are ultimately the agents responsible for individual and group behavior.

Sir Julian Huxley expressed the convictions of a growing number of biologists and social scientists when he wrote:

> *It is clear that for any major advance in national and international efficiency we can not depend on haphazard tinkering with social and political symptoms or ad hoc patching up of the world's political machinery, or even on improving education, but must rely increasingly on raising the genetic level of man's intellectual and practical abilities.*

Like Huxley, many scientists are becoming increasingly convinced that the problems lie not with the institutions humanity fashions, but with the way humanity itself is fashioned.

As succeeding generations become enamored with the many ways the genes can be manipulated, it is quite likely that biological technology will be rationalized with a new sociology and a new politic that are congenial with the wholesale genetic engineering of the human species.

Attempts to reform the internal blueprint of the human gene pool will raise the very real and frightening spectre of biological caste systems in every genetically controlled society. Societies have always been divided between the haves and the have-nots, the powerful and the powerless, the elite and the masses. Throughout history, people have been segregated by castes, with a myriad of rationales being used to justify the injustices of class division and exploitation. Race, religion, language, nationality are all well-worn methods for categorization and victimization. Now with the emergence of genetic engineering, society entertains the prospect of a new and more deadly form of segregation. The new prejudice will be based on genotype.

Increasingly in the decades and centuries to come, people will be categorized on the basis of their genetic make-up. Those families that can afford to program superior genetic traits into their fetuses at conception will assure their offspring a biological advantage, and thus a social advantage. One's economic role in society will be increasingly determined by one's genetic make-up. It is likely that individual genotypes will be increasingly matched with job opportunities as society embarks on a long journey to reorganize the body politic along genetic lines. This process has already begun. Over the past decade, many workers in the chemical industry have been genetically screened to match their chromosomes to their job description. According to one industrial observer, "the matching of genotype to job will someday be done routinely." In the genetically organized society of the future, political power will likely rest atop a biological caste system.

Segregating individuals by their genetic make-up represents a fundamental leap in the exercise of political power. In a society where the individual can be manipulated and constrained at conception by direct design of the blueprints of life, political power becomes more absolute and human freedom more elusive.

E.O. Wilson, the Harvard professor and founding father of sociobiology, speaks eloquently to the vision of a new order, one in which humanity takes on the task of redesigning itself in order that it might, in turn, effectively redesign the world in which it lives. In the final passage of his Pulitzer prize-winning book, *On Nature*, Wilson calls upon the species to assume the role of architect of the human species.

> *In time much knowledge concerning the genetic foundation of social behavior will accumulate, the techniques may become available for altering gene complexes by molecular engineering and rapid selection through cloning. . . . The human species can change its own nature. What will it choose? Will it remain the same, teetering on a gerrybuilt foundation of partly obsolete Ice-Age adaptations? Or will it press on toward still higher intelligence and creativity, accompanied by a greater – or lesser – capacity for emotional response? New patterns of sociality could be installed in bits and pieces. It might be possible to imitate genetically the more nearly perfect nuclear family of the white-handed gibbon or the harmonious sisterhoods of the honeybee.*

It is difficult for our generation even to imagine a society where political decisions are inspired by a genetic determinism. After all, we have been taught to believe that each person at birth is more or less a blank slate; that mind and consciousness is filled in by constant interaction with one's environment over a lifetime. Our children's generation and their children will grow up in a far different world. They will be much more comfortable with the idea of manipulating life from the genetic level. They will be caught up in a biotechnical web, organizing the stuff of life into the stuff of economic and social existence. Future generations will be at ease with the psychology of programming and engineering the human blueprint. Is there much doubt that the political philosophy of succeeding generations will more and more come to reflect their technological capabilities?

Very few people are entirely comfortable with the thought that the tools to redesign life are now within grasp. Perhaps that's why we are so uneasy about discussing eugenics. Even with all of the excitement being generated by the prospect of engineering life, we somehow sense the menacing outline of a eugenics shadow on the far-distant horizon. Still, we would find it exceedingly difficult to say no to a technological revolution that offers such an impressive array of benefits.

Thus we find ourselves ensnared on the horns of a dilemma as we make the first tentative moves into the Age of Biology. One part of us, our more ancient side, reels at the prospect of the further desacralizing of life, of reducing ourselves and all other sentient creatures to chemical codes to be manipulated for purely instrumental and utilitarian ends. Our other side, the side firmly entrenched in modernity, is zealously committed to bringing the biology of the planet in line with our most cherished new value, efficiency. It is our modernity that speaks so forcefully to us as we ponder the imponderable – the question of whether to engineer the life of the planet to conform with our desire for increased efficiency. It is our modern selves, dressed up in the philosophical garb of the Enlightenment, that provides comfort for our intentions and that shores up any nagging doubt we might have about the righteousness of the course we have set out before us.

The architects of modernity, the great seers of the Age of Progress, speak forcefully from the grave, beseeching us to take hold of the great task at hand. The words of Francis Bacon pierce through the veil of reservations we might have reminding us that the prime objective of the pursuit of knowledge is to advance our power over the forces of nature. Not to proceed with this revolution is unthinkable, as it would violate the very spirit of the human intellect; a spirit that knows no bounds in its restless search to wrest power and exercise greater control over the life force of the planet.

Could human consciousness bear to say no to the ultimate intellectual adventure, gaining access and control over the blueprints of life? Surely not. And what of the contention that such rank manipulation reduces all of life to pure utilitarianism? In the writings of the great social theorist, John Locke, we find an appropriate antidote for our troubled conscience. Such concerns are of little or no consequence. Utilitarianism is not something to apologize for, but something to revel in. The human being is, by nature, acquisitive and utilitarian. To negate nature, to subdue and harness it, to remake it in our own image, to use it for our own ends is to fulfill our destiny. Genetic technology represents the ultimate negation of nature. It is a final testimonial to the suspicion we've long entertained; that all of nature, all of the physical and biological world, has been put here for our exclusive use. To say no to the genetic engineering of life is to rob humanity of its rightful inheritance, its claim to sovereignty over the creation.

But is it unnatural to tinker in such a profound way with the biology of the planet? Not at all, if we just pause to recollect our thoughts about the natural scheme of things. Is nature itself not fluid and ever changing? Did not Darwin instruct us that creatures are continually recombining, mutating and metamorphosing into new species? Is not opportunism and utility the mechanism that ensures continued improvement in nature? Seen in this light, genetic engineering is little more than an amplification and speeding up of natural evolutionary development.

But don't we do a disservice to the sanctity of life when we reduce its meaning to information coded in the nucleic acid? Not really. We long ago accepted Descartes' picture of a mechanistic universe totally understandable in terms of mathematical logic. The only real difference in our perception today is that we view life more appropriately as being made up of information flows and computable programs rather than mechanistic parts. We still remain convinced, however, that we can quantify our way to the truth of existence. Genetic engineering, then, seems an altogether appropriate path for us to follow if we are to unravel the mysteries of life.

The genetic engineering revolution has already been legitimized, well before the institutions of political authority have even begun to affix their stamp of approval. This newest technological journey has received its blessing *de facto*. It has been consecrated by the culture and with great élan. Its swift acceptance is not difficult to understand. We have come to accept genetic technology as part of us because its logic, its objectives and its method of pursuit comport nicely with the world view we adhere to.

We now have a technology that promises to complete the vision first set forth by the scholars of the Enlightenment. These men of yesteryear challenged the medieval view that this was "the best of all possible worlds." They preferred a new vision, "that all worlds are possible." The French aristocrat, the Marquis de Condorcet, excited the passions of an age when he confidently proclaimed that:

> *No bounds have been fixed to the improvement of the human faculties . . . the perfectability of man is absolutely indefinite; . . . the progress of this perfectability, henceforth above the control of every power that would impede it, has no other limit than the duration of the globe upon which nature has placed us.*

Efficiency, progress, perfectibility. This is the rallying cry of the Genetic Age. The pressure to apply these standards to the genetic blueprints of the planet will be overwhelming. Indeed, to say no to perfecting the efficiency of biological systems will likely be treated as a mark of heresy and the gravest form of sin in the coming decades and centuries.

Who would dare oppose the engineering of new "super" plants and animals to feed a hungry world? Who would dare take exception to engineering new forms of biological energy to replace a dwindling reserve of fossil fuels? Who would dare protest the introduction of new microbes to eat up toxic wastes and other forms of chemical pollution? Who would dare object to genetic surgery to eliminate crippling diseases?

The short-term benefits of the emerging Biotechnical Age appear so impressive that any talk of curtailing or preventing their widespread application is likely to be greeted with incredulity, if not outright hostility.

How could anyone in good conscience oppose a technology that offers such hope for bettering the lot of humanity? To deny increased efficiency, progress and perfectibility is likely to be regarded as immoral, irresponsible and indefensible in the coming Genetic Age.

Is the genetics revolution to be considered a *fait accompli*? Is there no choice to make, except the rather narrow one of learning to live with and adjust to its central assumptions? Are we to see ourselves as the passive recipients of this profound technological change? Is there no reasonable alternative, no other approach to the future that might serve as a reprieve to the Genetics Age? Are we, in fact, locked in by a kind of historical determinism, destined to become both the architects of creation and the ultimate product of our own design?

Is the Genetics Revolution the inevitable next stage of the universal unfolding process, or a creature of our own immediate whims and caprices? Exactly how much say do we have in our future and the future life of the planet?

Part III

Declaration of a Heretic

• • •

In 1831, Western scientists discovered chloroform. Centuries earlier, Chinese scientists discovered acupuncture. Why did the Chinese never come upon chloroform as an anethesia? Why did the West never happen upon acupuncture? Is it likely that sooner or later each civilization might have independently discovered the scientific secrets of the other, even if they had continued to be geographically isolated? Most cultural anthropologists would argue that the chances of such a scientific coincidence were slim or non-existent. That's because both of these forms of anesthesia are products of the unique historical world view of each of these two great civilizations.

Europe and China entertained very different intellectual and theological traditions. Each relied on a very different set of underlying assumptions and principles in their pursuit of scientific knowledge. It is these assumptions and principles that established the broad context and the outer parameters for the kind of scientific breakthroughs that each civilization would come to claim as its unique historical contribution.

There is nothing inevitable about the introduction of new technologies into the life of a civilization. It might be well to remember that many highly advanced civilizations, of great sophistication and intellectual accomplishment, survived quite nicely without ever stumbling upon an invention as simple as the wheel. What a civilization discovers depends upon the conceptual framework it chooses to live by. In the West we chose to live by a world view that has led to the nuclear bomb and the engineering of the genetic blueprints of life. If this reality is less than comforting, it is even more disturbing to witness non-Western cultures rush to embrace both our scientific world view and the two powerful technologies that have been erected from it.

Still, there is also reason to hope that this emergent reality can be challenged and surmounted. But to have any possibility of succeeding, we must first be willing to cast aside the technological determinism that has so gripped the consciousness of the culture. There is nothing inevitable about the split atom or the engineered gene. The fact is, there is a future that lies beyond both of these technologies: a future wholly free of the consciousness that nurtured and sustains these powerful realities.

If this seems startling, it is understandable. The powers that be inform us that it is impossible to ever rid the idea of the bomb or genetic engineering from the thinking of the human race. They tell us that these discoveries can never be recalled, but, at best, only contained. They are wrong. The bomb and genetic engineering are not a fact of life like the coming and going of the seasons. They are inventions fashioned by human hands and conceived by the human mind. As such, they can be removed from both our culture and our consciousness.

For many this will be a shocking message, so conditioned have we become to thinking of these two technologies as the inexorable centerpiece and overriding reality of the coming age. The idea of eliminating the bomb and genetic engineering will be especially difficult to accept for those who have lost all hope of ever influencing their technological future. Many of our generation believe that their fate has already been consigned, and that nuclear holocaust or the Brave New World is to be their destiny. Our generation must realize that the future is never fated. It is always willed into existence.

If our generation desires a nuclear free future, and a future free of genetic engineering, it must will it with a strength of conviction that can tumble the walls of the old consciousness and lay the foundation for a new vision and a new order. It is human will that brings together thought and action, expectation and commitment, concept and implementation into a single force. It is human will that changes the world. It is human will that we now turn our attention to in our bid to redirect the future of our species away from nuclear Armageddon and a eugenic civilization.

• • •

10
Constructing a New World View

There is a new movement emerging in the intellectual community, one very different from the kinds that often capture the headlines in the daily press. This movement is not caught up in protests, legislation and votes. It is a very different type of movement, and in the long run, that is, the very long run, its success or failure could well help determine whether or not our species and the earth we're housed in will survive a holocaust.

The conspirators in this movement hardly know themselves. At times, they seem strangely unaware of the forces they are unleashing. Yet, their words and deeds pose a fundamental threat to our prevailing world view. If this rather disorganized band of intellectual dissidents succeed in transforming the disparate strands of their individual efforts into a fully conscious movement, their efforts could spark a new vision of the future for the human species to rally around.

The modern day heretics are to be found in the schoolrooms and university lecture halls of America. They are an in-between generation of teachers, professors and students caught up in a vast social time-warp, separating the material excesses of the 1950s from the grim realities of the 1980s. They were influenced, deeply touched and on occasion jolted by the powerful series of forces, movements and events that swept across the political landscape in the past two decades. Their perspective has been shaped by the civil rights movement, the war in Vietnam, the feminist movement, the right-to-life movement, the new Evangelical revival and the environmental movement. They are a new generation of scholars preparing to do battle against what is certainly a formidable foe. Their enemy is the consciousness of contemporary Western civilization.

This generation of scholars are preparing to do battle with the very way we human beings think. Not the day to day way we think: their interest is not in the thinking that characterizes a generation or an age, but rather the thinking that characterizes the species. Their effort is truely monumental and without parallel; to redirect the very consciousness of the human species, to chart a fundamental new path for the human mind.

This new breed of soldiers, these warriors of the mind, are inspired by a new sense of purpose. Their mission is to redefine our approach to knowledge, redirect our relationship to technology, reformulate our ideas about the nature of economic activity and re-establish a new framework for achieving security. Their goal, in short, is to disarm the world view that has given rise to the nuclear bomb and genetic engineering, and to lead the species back to the gates of Paradise by way of a new and largely unexplored route.

There is much talk today in big and small places about saving the world from extinction by redirecting the affairs of nations. But, if we are even to hope to do that, we must also talk about saving the human mind by redirecting the individual and collective consciousness of the human race. This is the end to which a small but growing number of people are dedicated. This is the story of their efforts to make the world a safer, more secure place to live in. Their story needs to be told, and retold until it is heard by everyone who still wants to hear. Its message is one of hope, of new beginnings.

The politics of a civilization are largely determined by the way it chooses to pursue knowledge, the way it chooses to use tools and the way it chooses to organize its economic activity. All of our ideas about "security" flow from the predispositions we hold in regard to these broad categories of human experience. Therefore, it we are to redefine the concept of security, we need to rethink our basic assumptions about the pursuit of knowledge, our relationship to technology, and the nature of the economic process.

11

Reconceptualizing Knowledge

Our consciousness has been so rooted in the idea that knowledge is power that we find it difficult to even imagine that there might exist another completely different way to exercise the human mind. Yet there is, as far as we can surmise, no firm rule etched into our psyche that requires that we use our consciousness solely as a weapon for capturing and controlling the world around us. It is conceivable to entertain another approach to the pursuit of knowledge: one that would fundamentally change the very basis of sociality. Instead of pursuing knowledge to gain power and control, we could just as well pursue knowledge to experience empathy and participation. Instead of using knowledge to increase our rule over, we might just as easily use knowledge to become a partner with the rest of the earthly creation.

With the old form of knowledge our interest is always focused on knowing how things manifest themselves so that we can use, exploit, harness and control them. In the exercise of this particular approach to knowledge, we separate ourselves from everything in the environment around us in order that we might then turn all things into objects to be manipulated, used or consumed. It is this basic alienation that drags us further and further away from our first home, that beatific estate where no differentiation existed, where there was no awareness of self and other. Where all was harmony.

In contrast, empathetic knowledge reaches out in a very different way. The mind is not interested in controlling but rather in connecting. With this new approach to knowledge we are constantly asking about the many ways in which we are related to everything else. We seek to identify with the things around us, to recognize ourselves in the other and the other in ourselves. Our goal is to join with, to become one with all of the rest of creation. To "know," under this new schema, is to know how to participate with our surroundings rather than how to control them.

Architecture provides a convenient metaphor for describing these two very different approaches to the pursuit of knowledge. Many contemporary architects dream of building a skyscraper; a monument of invincibility that can stand self-contained and isolated, jutting above its surroundings in princely relief. They are always in search of new building materials, new tools and new principles of organization that will allow them to build a fortress that can withstand and survive all possible assaults from the environment. For the architects of skyscrapers, the knowledge pursued is the knowledge of how to maximize power and control over the environment. Their works of art are designed to imperialize their environment, to expropriate and devour their surroundings. Consider for a moment the fact that the Sears Roebuck Tower in Chicago, the world's tallest building, uses up more energy resources in a given twenty-four-hour day than the entire city of Rockford, Illinois, with 147,000 people living in it.

Then there are the new architects whose approach to knowledge is guided by very different considerations. They dream of building a passive solar home that is so elegant and inobtrusive, so meshed with its natural environment, that it is difficult to even distinguish where their work of art leaves off and the works of nature begin. Their interest is in developing materials, tools and principles of design that are compatible with the environment they are involved with. They see their buildings not as a fortress, but as an environment within an environment; an extension of their surroundings that fully participates with the rhythms, beats and periodicities of its larger setting. Their buildings participate with the heat and light of the sun, the cycles of the seasons, the geography of the land and the currents and tides of the winds and water. Their buildings belong to the environment. For these architects, the knowledge pursued is the knowledge of how to empathize and be a participant with the world.

These two types of architects express two very different views of security in their pursuit of knowledge. For the designer of skyscrapers, security comes from building an impenetrable turret, a structure that can control and dominate its surroundings. For the designer of the passive solar home, security comes from building a structure that can become part of a larger already well established community, the ecosystem.

In every branch of learning, a new generation of students and teachers are challenging the orthodox notion of controlling knowledge with the radically different idea of empathetic knowledge. For example, in the biology department, the genetic engineers are asking the "how" of nature so that we can design more efficient, more commerciably viable forms of life. On the other hand, there are the ecologists who, in glaring contrast, are seeking to identify with the subtle relationships and interactions between all living things, so that we can better learn how to integrate the social and economic rhythms of society with the biological rhythms of the rest of the living kingdom.

In the engineering departments, there are physicists working on elaborate nuclear fusion reactors, attempting to harness a storehouse of energy more powerful than the sun to give us even greater control over the environment than we have now. Then, there are the other breed of physicists who are working with wind, solar and water power, in an effort to develop appropriate technologies that are empathetic to and congenial with the rhythms and flows of the natural environment.

In medical schools the standard approach to health care is still based on the idea of getting control over the immediate environment where a problem exists. Oftentimes the body is treated like a machine that needs repair. In the process the medical care is often cold, mechanical and unfeeling. The doctors become more and more detached from the patients, to the point where little, if any, physical contact exists between the two. In place of the warm caring touch of another human being, the patient is molested, scanned, probed and screened by an impersonal array of highly sophisticated machines.

Yet, even in medicine, there are signs that a new empathetic approach to knowledge is emerging as a viable alternative. The holistic health movement emphasizes a nurturing, participating interaction between practitioner and patient, and calls upon the latter to identify with their own bodily rhythms and to work with, instead of against, the illness. The body is not treated in isolation but rather as an integral part of the larger environment that it is in constant participation with. The emphasis is on letting the entire environment assist in helping to restore the proper functioning relationships of the body.

An empathetic approach to medical treatment places greater attention on prevention over cure. For example, consider the two major diseases that confront industrial society today: cancer and heart disease. While these diseases have always existed, they have assumed epidemic proportions in the past several decades. A host of clinical studies point to a strong causal relationship between the poor nutrition, high-stress, carcinogenic environment we have created and the triggering of these particular diseases. The empathetic school of medicine focuses its research on finding ways to eliminate the source of the problem. Concern is directed toward cleaning up the polluted environment, and helping to change the nutritional habits and personal hygiene of the individual members of society.

This approach is in stark contrast to the more traditional forms of medicine which leave the "source" of the problem unattended, concentrating instead on surgical intervention, and in the future gene intervention, in order that people may continue to live in the polluted, high-stress environment that helps trigger the diseases in the first place.

In all of the areas just touched on, and in regard to countless other examples that one might easily cite, it is apparent that the human mind is beginning to look out onto the world with a very different set of lenses. A new approach to knowledge is beginning to take shape.

For a long time, the proponents of controlling knowledge have chastized those who dared to challenge their form of reasoning by accusing them of obstructing the free flow of knowledge and of stifling freedom of inquiry. If theirs was the only approach to the pursuit of knowledge available to the human mind, then their protestations would be more than justified. But such is not the case. One can be deeply and irreconcilably opposed to the dominant form of knowledge being pursued in the world today, and still champion the principle of progress and the unimpeded expansion of human consciousness. Certainly, the pursuit of empathetic knowledge is every bit as intellectually challenging, as invigorating and stimulating to the human mind as the pursuit of controlling knowledge. In fact, one could well argue that if there is any real obstacle in the way of the future development of the collective mind of the species, it is to be found in the traditional approach to knowledge we have been relying on for so long. This kind of knowledge has resulted in a cascading pyramid of technological and social crises, one heaped on top of another, with the nuclear bomb and genetic engineering now perched on the apex, threatening the extinction of consciousness itself. Can there be any greater threat to free and open inquiry than an approach to knowledge which each day tightens its stranglehold on the survival of the species? It is this approach to knowledge that has all but run its course; its demise dimly perceived in the shadow of the first mushroom cloud wafting its way over the ancient Japanese countryside.

Still, time and again we fall back on the notion that progress, freedom of inquiry and the development of both the nuclear bomb and genetic engineering are somehow inextricably intermeshed. That is one of the reasons why it is so very hard to entertain the idea of rejecting these new super technologies.

Our mind reels at such a prospect. Impossible, we say. The idea itself can never be recalled. The genie can never be put back into the bottle. To attempt to do so would be futile. And herein lies the source of the great despair that hovers over our civilization. It is that haunting sense that it is too late, that we cannot erase what has come to pass, that there is nothing to do but wait in quiet resignation, hoping, at best, to buy a bit more time for ourselves and perhaps our children.

Because we know of no other way to think, it is easy to see how we would come to this state of mind regarding nuclear technology and genetic engineering. For if it is of the essence of the human mind to seek power and control over the environment and each other, then these two great technologies surely represent the final flowering of human consciousness. After all, do they not represent the ultimate exercise of power and control over the forces of nature?

If human consciousness is by nature controlling, then the only way to rid the world of the bomb and genetic engineering is to legislate the human mind out of existence. Short of that, it is inevitable that the human mind will continue to imagine, conceptualize and build upon both these technologies. It will simply be unable to do anything else because as long as it is allowed to function, it will think of how to exercise control over the environment – and as long as it thinks of how to exercise control over the environment, it will think about the construction of bigger and better bombs and the designing of more efficient biological organisms.

This then, is the sickly fear that underlies all others; the root of the great malaise that has immobilized the species. What if the idea behind both these ultimate technologies is not just an unfortunate accident of history but the highest expression of the consciousness of the race?

In order to reject this grimmest of all thoughts, we would have to be willing to reject the idea that the overriding purpose of the conscious mind is to seek control over its environment. We would have to be willing to consider the possibility of pursuing a different knowledge path: one designed not to control the environment but to empathize with it.

This is not much to ask in return for the continuation of the species and the planet. Certainly the human mind has shown itself capable of fulfilling such a mandate. Time and again the individual and the society have demonstrated a passionate willingness to pursue this alternate path. To be sure, the moments of commitment have been fleeting. These empathetic interludes always seem to appear quite suddenly, like a tracer light brightening up the dark skies of the mind for a passing instant, only to be just as quickly dissipated as the human consciousness hurriedly readjusts to its more controlling orientation.

It is possible, then, for the mind to think in a radically different way. The issue is not whether we can redirect the collective consciousness of the species, but whether we have the zeal to sustain such a concerted effort over a period of time.

It is not our imagination that is holding us back from a grand new vision of our place and purpose in the world. Rather, it is the expectation we have about ourselves. We prefer to fall back on the cliché that human beings have always been aggressive and controlling and that it is impossible to change the very nature of the species. Of course, no one would deny that this is the side of human behavior that has dominated the affairs of society for as far back as anyone cares to remember. But, it is also true that the other side of human behavior has also made its imprint from time to time: the side that puts the sacredness of life before all other considerations.

In the final analysis it is our expectation about the nature of our species that is likely to determine our fate. If we continue to think of ourselves as inherently aggressive and controlling, then on what basis could we ever convincingly challenge those individuals or nations who choose to fulfill their biological destiny by building more controlling forms of weaponry, or by exercising power over the biological blueprints of life?

If, on the other hand, we come to think of ourselves as inherently empathetic to all other life and to the environment that nurtures life, then we would be more than justified in condemning those who would violate those canons of human behavior, and in preventing them from building more bombs or from manipulating the genetic codes of living things on this planet.

Whether we survive or perish as a species, then, will depend largely on how we choose to define ourselves. It's as simple and as complicated as that. But at least, let it not be said that we have no choice, that our fate is sealed, that there is no recourse. There is. The choice of whether we live or die is in our hands. If we choose to live, we must find the inner strength, the reserve, to undo the years of cynicism and self-doubt, the years of fear and resignation that have so stymied us.

We have long sought knowledge to obtain power, to gain control, to become secure. Now that kind of pursuit has put us within minutes of our own termination. Is it not time for the world to acknowledge that there is nothing more to be gained by this type of knowledge? We have used it up, and it has failed us. It has led us farther and farther away from the security we yearn for.

The fact of the matter is that we have reached the end of the line for a method of human inquiry that has accompanied us from the first day of our journey into human consciousness. With each passing day, this long-relied-on form of reasoning appears more stilted, more tautological, more tiresome. Though we are naturally reluctant to part with a way of thinking that has been, for so long, the defining characteristic of the species, it is becoming painfully evident that any further reliance on this form of knowledge would be self-defeating for the human race.

As to the empathetic approach to knowledge, it beckons us forth into areas barely touched on by the human mind. It offers us unexplored opportunities. It opens up new avenues for the mind to play in. It is an untried method of inquiry that poses fresh challenges for the human race. With an empathetic approach to knowledge we begin to retrain ourselves in a new catechism. In place of the adage that knowledge is power, power is control and control is security, we begin to exercise the human mind with the thought that knowledge is empathy, empathy is participation and participation is security. In the new scheme of consciousness, security is achieved by becoming an integral participant in the larger communities of life that make-up the single organism we call earth. Security is no longer to be found in self-contained isolation but rather in shared partnership with the creation. Security is not to be found in dominating and manipulating, but rather in reweaving ourselves back into the web of relationships that make up the earthly and cosmic ecosystems.

It is time to let the whole world know that there is a new way to think about security, a new way to think about the pursuit of knowledge, and a new way to think about the nature and purpose of thought itself. To free the human mind, to let it choreograph new patterns for the species, to let it roam into new domains where it can excite with visions never before dreamed of. This is the great healing task that stretches out before us, and that gives us, our children and their children, something noble to aspire to.

12
Redefining our Relationship to Technology

Changing the way we think also means changing the way we think about the tools we make and use. There is a subtle irony in the way we have come to think of our technology. On the one hand we look to it as our salvation in times of crisis. Having relegated God to the role of a disinterested cosmic bystander, we have only our faith in our tools to hold on to when all else fails us. During the bad times, when hope itself seems in such short supply, we comfort ourselves with the thought that somewhere, somehow, there is someone tinkering with a new gadget, tool or machine, and that soon this new contraption will be rushed in to rescue us from the malaise that engulfs us. In a world fractured by ideologies and conflicting loyalties, there still remains a single-minded devotion on the part of all industrialized peoples toward the technological fruits.

Nowhere is this more apparent than in the nuclear arms race, where technology is being looked to as a last hope to ward off the unthinkable. The President, the Congress, the military strategists are in frantic pursuit of a new generation of weapons that can effectively counteract those we've already developed. The public is being fed an incessant barrage of military propaganda concerning the latest development in lasers, particle beams, killer satellites and other new space-age weapons, always with the caveat that these new weapons systems will provide us with a nearly fail-safe means of defending ourselves against the current crop of weapons on hand. Our answer, then, to the deepening crisis brought on largely by the technology we have fashioned, is to fashion even more technology, never once stopping to consider that the problem might reside in the solution.

Of course, pure faith is often blind to even the most obvious of contradictions. When it comes to our belief in the magical qualities of technology, our other sensibilities become dulled in the presence of the unqualified allegiance we so willingly extend. The fact is, we imbue our technological prowess with Godlike qualities.

On the other hand, we always seem to feel a bit uncomfortable with the sycophantic relationship we have adopted toward our technology. Part of us recoils at the thought that we might become overly dependent on our own machines. So we maintain the pretension that all our tools are neutral, and that they only become agents of power when endowed for specific tasks by their creators. The long-standing fiction is that tools have no inherent value built into them, but only reflect the values of the people who use them.

This is a false conception. False and dangerous. By harboring the illusion that all our technologies are neutral, we never have to accept the responsibility of having to say no to the development of a single one of them. But technologies aren't neutral. There has never been a neutral technology. All technologies are power. A lance gives us more projectile power than our throwing arm. An automobile gives us more locomotive power than our legs and feet. A teleconference provides us with more communication power than is possible through face to face interaction. The purpose of every technology is to somehow enhance our well-being. Technologies, by their very nature, are expropriating; they extract, they distill, they process, they organize, they convert, they consume, they regiment. Technologies change the equation of nature by giving human beings a distinct advantage over each other and the other species. With our technologies we inflate ourselves beyond our natural biological limits with the help of artificial limbs and extensions.

Tools are power. Each and every tool we use has power built into it by the very nature of the task is was designed for. Every time we use a tool to enhance our well-being, it is an indisputable fact that our gain can only be at the expense of a loss somewhere else. The exercise of power necessitates that for every victory there must be a defeat, for every increase, a diminution. That is the nature of power. The tools we create are saturated with power because their whole reason for being is to provide us with "an advantage."

The question, then, that has not yet been seriously addressed before the counsels of world public opinion is this. If all technologies are power, then how much power is appropriate? Is it possible to conceive of a technology with so much built-in power that it would be inappropriate to use it, or even continue to make it?

Up to now we have argued that there is never really any appropriate time and place to say no to any new technology. That's because the human mind has long regarded every new technological means of exerting control over the environment to be appropriate. As long as we pursue knowledge in order to gain more and more power over the environment and each other, why would we ever willingly say no to any new tool our mind conceives to advance that end?

Even those who are often regarded as the most vocal critics of new technological advances are likely to contend that the problem lies not with the technology we create, but with the people who control it. There are many among us who still believe that if all technology is democratized and put in the hands of the people, it will be socially transformed and be used only for good purposes. For these people, the question is never whether to accept or reject a new technology, but only how to regulate and control it. They fail to see that a nuclear reactor in a perfectly organized socialist state will perform no differently than a nuclear reactor in the most capitalist country.

Setting our minds free from the old way of thinking about technology will not be easy. It will require an acknowledgement on our part that some technologies ought not to be used under any circumstances, because what they do threatens either the sacred quality of life or the survivability of life. Certain technologies are so inherently powerful that, in the mere act of using them, we do damage to ourselves and our environment.

It is time to develop a new set of tools that are empathetic to the environment they are used in: tools that cajole rather than grab; tools that select rather than pillage; tools that operate at a speed commensurate with the rhythms, beats and tempo of the environments they are engaged in. Appropriate technologies are technologies that are congenial with their surroundings, that create the least amount of disturbance, and that are used sparingly enough to insure that the environment can be allowed to replenish itself.

Controlling technologies and empathetic technologies manifest two very different ideas about the nature of security. With controlling technologies, the emphasis is on maximizing present opportunities. With empathetic technologies the emphasis is on maximizing future possibilities. With controlling technologies, a high premium is placed on optimizing efficiency for the present generation. With empathetic technologies, a high premium is placed on maintaining an endowment for future generations.

Agriculture provides a good example of these two contrasting modes of technology at work. The high-technology farmers are constantly engaged in the pursuit of new, more exotic forms of plant and soil manipulation to exercise greater control over the forces of nature. For them, agriculture has become a battleground for introducing more sophisticated weapons, in the form of chemical fertilizers and pesticides, in an effort to exact as great a tribute as possible from the soil and plants under cultivation. In high-technology agriculture, the emphasis is on maximizing crop yield in the minimum amount of time. By infusing an array of laboratory produced chemicals into the soil and by manipulating the genetic make-up of the plants to create more homogenous strains, it is possible to dramatically increase yield in the short run, but at the expense of the erosion and depletion of the soil base and a severe loss of genetic diversity in the plants in the long run.

In contrast, organic farmers are developing a sophisticated store of knowledge about the delicate balance of relationships that govern the plant cycles, are introducing organic fertilizers and natural pest controls, and are paying close attention to restoring the natural rhythms of production and recycling. Organic farmers see their role as nurturing rather than marshalling. Their concern is to preserve the soil base and the natural plant strains in order to insure an adequate reserve for future generations to share. In the short run, the organic farmers are likely to get less yield than the high technology farmers. In the long run, their overall yield will be much higher because they allowed the soil and the plants to replenish themselves over many cycles and seasons.

An empathetic approach to technology starts with the assumption that everything is interrelated and dependent on everything else for its survival, and that technological intervention should be minimized in order to do the least damage to the myriad relationships that exist in the natural world. There is an acknowledgement that some form of expropriation is always necessary. All things desire to live, and it is a law of nature that for something to live, something else must die. But it is also true that too much expropriation can result in destroying the very life support systems we rely on for our future survival. There is a distinction to be made, then, between mutual give and take, which exists in every set of relationships, and the kind of blind expropriation that strains and eventually severs the relationships altogether.

13
Rethinking Economics

If, as Locke, Smith and the other philosophers of the modern era contend, continued growth and greater efficiency are the keys to improving the lot of the individual and the security of the society, then the more we grow and the more efficient we become, the more secure we will be as a society. By this line of reasoning, the only way to assure our continued security is to expropriate, transform and consume the earth's resources faster and faster. Today, every society on the planet accepts the logic of this central assumption concerning the nature of security and, as a result, the nations of the world find themselves locked into a fierce competition for territory, resources and labor pools. In the mad dash to control and consume the resources of the earth, every nation is expanding its military arsenals, stockpiling weapons, and maintaining vast standing armies. Nations are threatening, blackmailing, invading and occupying neighboring lands to exact advantage. Every country is committed to growth and expansion, and is using every military means at its disposal to obtain the necessary power to advance these ends. Ironically, all of this rivalry, this competition, this expropriation and exploitation is being done in the name of security. With each new day, the world becomes more embattled and the prospect of survival more problematical, and still the powers that be continue to tout the idea that continued growth and expansion are the only ways to achieve a lasting security.

If we are ever to hope to reverse the spiral of imperialism and militarism that the nations of the world have embarked upon, we will have to redefine the nature of security by redefining the nature of economic activity. That redefinition begins with a fundamental change in terminology. Our generation can reshape our ideas about security by substituting the term "borrowing" for the term "growth" in our economic thinking.

The most important truth about ourselves, our artifacts and our civilization is that it is all borrowed. Even the molecules in our face and body are there only temporarily, on their journey to and from the environment. We are forever borrowing from the environment to create and maintain the totality of our way of life. We borrow resources from nature and transform them into utilities in order to gain some temporary measure of economic well-being. Everything we transform eventually ends up back in nature after we have expropriated whatever temporary value we can from it. The moment we introduce the idea of borrowing into economics a sense of responsibility suddenly enters the picture, because with borrowing comes the notion of indebtedness. If every aspect of our survival depends on borrowing, then we are indebted to the core of our being. Implicit in the concept of borrowing and debt is the idea of paying back. Borrowing then, has built-in limits. One should borrow only to the extent that one can pay back. A civilization should borrow only to the extent it can pay back.

To acknowledge indebtedness is to accept the idea that we owe our being, our very survival, to the many living and non-living things that had to be sacrificed in order for us to perpetuate ourselves.

Imagine what a vast change in economic thinking would attend a change from the politics of growth to the politics of borrowing. Gross National Product would become a measure of the temporary economic value we've expropriated at the expense of the resources we've used up and the wastes we've accumulated. We would begin to understand that the ultimate balancing of budgets is always between society and nature. The politics of borrowing would establish a new bottom-line principle: that society should never consume faster than nature can reproduce if it is to avoid the ultimate deficit, the depletion of the resource base that society depends on to maintain its economic activity.

If borrowing becomes the accepted way of understanding the

nature of the economic process, then every political and social decision must be judged by the impact it will have on maintaining the long-term balance between society's economic needs and desires and nature's reproductive capacity. Likewise, borrowing assumes a mutual give and take between parties. With borrowing comes the idea of relationship and interdependency. With indebtedness comes the idea of responsibility and accountability. By making the idea of borrowing the centerpiece of our economic vocabulary, we begin to entertain the notion of economics as a communal affair, in which everyone becomes responsible for each other and for the web of economic dependency that entwines them into a deep and integrated relationship with the larger environment.

Once we come to see ourselves as part of an indivisible whole, in which every living thing is accountable and indebted to every other living thing for its existence, the very idea of making war will become obsolete. For to make war, within this newly defined context, would be to make war on oneself. It is only by severing the idea of the binding relationship of all things that war is conceivable.

If the nuclear bomb has taught us anything, it is that we are, in fact, bound together in an inseparable web of dependency, and that any attempt to break-out from the labyrinth of mutual obligations that unite us not only imperils those immediately engaged in competitive struggle, but everyone else as well. The idea of sharing more equitably the fruits of our labor, of cooperating with our fellow human beings and with neighboring peoples, of showing a proper regard for the larger ecosystems that we inhabit, used to be regarded as impractical and naive. Now such thinking is absolutely essential if we are to continue to survive as a species.

Changing world views means changing basic assumptions about how we choose to organize ourselves and the world around us. Do we use the human mind to seek power over the forces of nature, or to empathize with the rest of the living kingdom? Do we use technology to maximize our advantage over the environment and each other, or to establish an equitable give-and-take relationship between all living things? Do we define economic activity in terms of growth and unlimited expansion, or in terms of borrowing and maintaining a proper regard for nature's ability to replenish itself? Do we define security as exercising greater control over our surroundings, or as participation in the larger communities of life that make up the ecosystems of the planet?

Within the old conceptual frame, it is impossible ever to conceive of a nuclear free world or a world without genetic engineering. As long as we continue to believe that our security can only be won by maximizing power, advantage, growth and control, we will never be able to give up nuclear weapons or the genetic engineering of life. It is only by radically rethinking our ideas about the nature of security that we can begin to imagine a world without the ever-present reality of these two technologies. By exchanging empathy for power, equity for advantage, borrowing and indebtedness for growth and expansion, and participation and caring for control and manipulation we establish a new reference point for insuring the security of each individual and the species as a whole. There is no room for nuclear weapons or genetic engineering in a world that defines itself as a single family, living in a single community, inhabiting a common ecosystem, enclosed in a single globe.

14
Making Peace with the Planet

Hegel once remarked that "weapons are nothing but the essence of the combatants themselves. . . ." In this essay we have traced the source of our nuclear and genetic nightmare to the way we think and we have, along the way, examined a wholly new way of thinking that offers an antidote for our tormented minds and our crisis-ridden culture. Now there remains one final consideration if we are successfully to make the jump from the old way of thinking to the new. It is time to entertain the ultimate heresy: to consider the idea of renouncing the use of power as a means of obtaining security.

Unfortunately, the question of rejecting the use of force has been too narrowly circumscribed to the geo-political realm. The question is not whether we are prepared to give up power to the Soviets, but whether we are prepared to repudiate the idea of power itself. The reason we can't give up our nuclear arms and our new genetic engineering technologies is because we still lack the commitment to give up our drive for control over the total environment we live in. That is why the idea of renouncing the use of power is so unacceptable, and why it fills us with fear to even contemplate such a prospect. Yet, it is obvious that until we are ready to cast aside our overriding preoccupation with exercising power over the world, we will be forever mired in an ever-expanding technological race that can only lead to the ultimate destruction of the biological and physical environment we live in.

Whenever someone raises the question of disarmament, the immediate rejoinder is likely to be, "Would you rather we surrender?" Up to now, each generation has been rendered mute whenever the discussion reached this critical impasse. But, what if our generation was willing to break the impasse? We might explain that the issue is not whether we are willing to surrender to the Russians. After all, even if the Russians ceased to be a perceived threat, there is no doubt we'd find some other hostile force to take their place. As long as our mind continues to view the world as a hostile place that needs to be controlled, there will be no end to the spiral of madness we've unleashed. Is it not possible that our generation might do what our parents' generation were too cowardly to do: renounce the exercise of power as a means of dealing with other nations?

There is great strength in the idea of repudiating the use of force. It is the strength of opposites, and it is the only option strong enough to deter both the nuclear arms race, and the race into the Brave New World.

The thought of rejecting the use of power triggers such a heated emotional reaction precisely because it is the opposite of control. If our generation can succeed in transforming the concept of renouncing power from one of weakness to one of strength, we will have discovered the source of our liberation.

The great challenge that lies before our generation is to recognize the path to our own freedom. We will need to understand that to renounce power is not to give up. It is to let go. It is to free ourselves at long last from the weight that has for so long shackled the consciousness of the species.

Some will wonder aloud as to whether an empathetic consciousness can succeed in a world still largely dominated by a power-seeking mind. They fail to see that the very act of repudiating the old consciousness and embracing the new is the victory, the most impressive victory one could ever hope to claim. It is impossible to control a mind that refuses to cooperate, that will not acknowledge the underlying assumptions governing the pursuit of power.

If one believes in their heart and soul that their own security resides not in control but in vulnerability, not in domination but in participation, then by what possible threat could they be made a victim? Certainly, the threat of loss of security would fall on deaf ears because their ideas about security flow from a very different set of assumptions. The traditional notion is that loss of security means loss of control, the inability to exercise power over one's environment. For one who had already made a voluntary choice to renounce control and the exercise of power over the environment, any attempt to take away such control or power would be redundant and unnecessary. Power can only be successfully exercised if there are willing participants: those who choose to take part either as victimizers or victims. If enough people choose not to cooperate with the exercise of power, that power eventually evaporates. Without popular support, or complicity or at least passive acceptance, the exercise of power is an impossibility.

Herein lies the most important single lesson our generation could learn. By the mere act of letting go of the drive for power, one automatically cancels the exercise of that drive by others, whether they be individuals or nations. This is not a new lesson. It is, in fact, the most ancient of all lessons and it has been taught to us countless times by the great prophetic teachers of history. Jesus renounced the exercise of power on the cross at Calvary. He turned the other cheek. He chose to be vulnerable when he could have dominated. And in a final act of empathy, he asked God to forgive his executioners. His crucifixion stands as the greatest testimonial in history to the strength that is to be found in an empathetic consciousness.

The story of Jesus confronts the consciousness as well as the conscience of the human race as no other event before or since. This simple carpenter from Galilee set a unique example for the rest of the species. He showed his brethren a new way to think, a new way to relate to the world. At times, even his own disciples were unable to comprehend the import of his message. They were so steeped in a controlling consciousness that his demands upon them to surrender, to be vulnerable and exposed seemed strangely capricious. When an armed mob descended on him in the garden that fateful night of his arrest, his disciple Peter besought his master to fight back. Jesus refused and chided Peter for taking up arms. In words that have since become the watch cry of all those who have chosen to surrender a controlling consciousness, Jesus warned that "all who take the sword will perish by the sword."

Jesus' mission was to teach a different way. Here was this man who claimed to be the son of God but who allowed his fellow human beings to persecute him and finally to kill him. Jesus could have chosen to exercise his superior power and wrest control from those who threatened him, but he chose not to. In so doing, he demonstrated for all future generations the great strength of both surrendering power and refusing to cooperate with those still exercising it.

> *You have heard that it was said, "an eye for an eye and a tooth for a tooth." But I say to you, do not resist one who is evil. But if any strikes you on the right cheek, turn to him the other also; and if anyone would sue you and take your coat, let him have your cloak as well; and if anyone forces you to go one mile, go with him two miles. Give to him who begs from you, and do not refuse him who would borrow from you. You have heard that it was said, "You shall love your neighbor and hate your enemy." But I say to you, love your enemies and pray for those who persecute you.*

For two thousand years these words have haunted the human consciousness. Each generation has been called forth to renounce mastery and control over the world. And in every generation there have been those select few who have chosen to take up the new covenant vision Jesus offered the world.

In our own time, it was the son of Hindu parents, a British educated barrister, that reconsecrated the vision. Mahatma Gandhi considered himself a simple man of the people. Yet Albert Einstein once said of this simple man that "generations to come will scarce believe that such a one as this ever in flesh and blood walked upon this earth."

Gandhi was a freedom fighter. He dedicated his life to liberating the Indian people from the yoke of British colonialism. But what made him so completely unique is the revolutionary philosophy he expounded and acted on. This frail, soft-spoken ascetic took on the most powerful Empire on earth by preaching the gospel of non-violent surrender. He urged his countrymen to refuse to cooperate with the forces of power and his countrymen took heed.

Gandhi's appeal ignited the passion of an entire people, but it was a very different kind of passion than was being unleashed in other countries where people were taking up arms to free themselves from the humiliation of colonial rule.

In India, people armed themselves with the dual philosophy of non-violence and non-cooperation. They simply refused to either fight or cooperate with their rulers. "The force generated by non-violence," said Gandhi, "is greater than the force of all the arms invented by man's ingenuity." And so, they marched through the cities, they petitioned the government, they sat down on the roads, they engaged in strikes at the workplace, and in the end, they brought the Empire to its knees. They stood together as a people and they were victorious. They found strength in vulnerability, dignity in surrender, and a common bond in their respect for the sanctity of life.

Gandhi reawakened the empathetic consciousness of his people. But the task was not easily accomplished. His detractors were quick to chide him for promulgating a philosophy of defeatism. There were many who equated non-violence with either passivity or cowardice. It is neither, Gandhi said. On the question of passivity, Gandhi counseled his critics that non-violence "does not mean meek submission to the will of the evil-doer, but it means the pitting of one's whole soul against the will of the tyrant. Working under this law of our being it is possible for a single individual to defy the whole might of an unjust empire . . . and lay the foundation for that empire's fall. . . ." On the question of cowardice, Gandhi remarked that, on the contrary, the fully armed man is more at heart a coward. "Possession of arms implies an element of fear, if not cowardice. But true non-violence is an impossibility without the possession of unadulterated fearlessness."

Gandhi's lasting triumph lies not in any specific end he was able to achieve. In the long history of human affairs, the liberation of a country from foreign domination is not in itself sufficient to inspire the thankful praise of future generations. Gandhi's triumph lies in the means he chose to secure the human welfare. He called on his countrymen and women to choose a different path to security. He asked them not only to renounce power over each other but also to accept responsibility for each other. And they responded; by the millions they responded. Gandhi liberated the long-imprisoned empathetic consciousness of the race.

It is this liberation of the human consciousness, far more

than the liberation of a country, that signals the greatness of the Gandhian moment. What makes the events in India so compelling is the image of a hundred million Gandhi supporters committed to a new way of thinking about the world and their relationship to it.

Gandhi said, "I have not the shadow of a doubt that any man or woman can achieve what I have, if he or she would make the same effort and cultivate the same hope and faith." Gandhi was an ordinary little man, who might just as easily have remained an anonymous number among those of his generation, were it not for his dogged determination to battle the conventional way of thinking with a new way of looking at the world. What made his contribution unique was his ability to enlist a similar commitment from other ordinary people like himself. Gandhi once remarked that "the religion of non-violence is not meant merely for the . . . saints. It is meant for the common people as well." Gandhi fervently believed in the capacity of the human will to make choices. He proved in his own life that every human being can make of themselves what they choose. We are not, in the final analysis, a prisoner of fate or our own consciousness. The great strength of the human species is to be found in our unique capacity to will our own future. In surveying the meaning of being human, Gandhi concluded that:

> *Man often becomes what he believes himself to be. If I keep on saying to myself that I can not do a certain thing, it is possible that I may end by really becoming incapable of doing it. On the contrary, if I have the belief that I can do it, I shall surely acquire the capacity to do it even if I may not have it at the beginning.*

There have been others in this century like Gandhi. We have had our Martin Luther Kings, and Mother Theresas. It is their names we remember, but we must also remember that these great people did not travel alone. Millions more of our race have committed themselves, some for a brief moment, others for a lifetime, to the awakening of an empathetic consciousness. Nor is our century unique. The human saga is punctuated by the presence of empathetic souls, men and women who have tried to steer a different course for themselves and the human race. Men and women who have refused to believe that a controlling consciousness is the only way to define the species. By their very presence they have shown that another future is possible to both imagine and experience.

Some might wonder why there is any reason to hope that our generation will be any more responsive to the call for a rebirth of human consciousness than all of the generations that preceded us. After all, why should we be expected to rise to a higher calling when others did not?

Perhaps the one thing that so separates our place in history from our parents and all of their ancestral kin is the all-pervasive threat of total annihilation. This possibility has never before existed for the human race. In the past, the species was more than willing to continue with the fiction that knowledge is power and that power is security, because there was always the expectation that one could exact some kind of advantage by exercising a controlling consciousness. That fiction is fast fading as we enter into the second millennium AD, with the specter of the complete democratization of nuclear war technology.

The universalization of the bomb has effectively destroyed the central assumption of controlling consciousness: that it is possible to gain some kind of advantage by pursuing power over all things. In the nuclear age, everyone's power represents a disadvantage to both themselves and the objects they seek to control. Because this is the case, we are likely to be the first generation in history to seriously consider the idea that more power means less security. For us, the old controlling consciousness seems more like a cruel joke we have perpetrated on ourselves than a reasonable approach to obtaining security.

The anti-nuclear movement often relies on a simple but effective analogy to point out the utter bankruptcy of the traditional approach to security. They ask us to imagine two people in a closed room, neck high in gasoline. One person has six matches, the other only three. Does the one with six matches have any reason to feel more secure by dint of the extra fire power at his disposal? Will the one with three matches feel any more secure if he obtains three more matches? Unfortunately, many of our policy leaders fervently believe that the only way to insure our security is to continue to provide more matches. Our political and military leaders are still vehemently committed to the "balance of terror" doctrine. The idea behind the balance of terror concept is that the super powers are two forces each attempting to tilt the finely balanced pendulum of nuclear superiority to their side. As long as each power is able to effectively offset each new weapons build-up of the other, with its own build-up, the nuclear pendulum will remain balanced. Neither side will gain an advantage over the other, and consequently, neither will risk nuclear blackmail or attempted aggression. Both sides believe that this balance of terror strategy will continue to insure a reasonable measure of predictability and security, regardless of the number of weapons that are produced.

The idea of the finely balanced pendulum is so much a part of the world view of the military strategists that most are unable to imagine any other way of thinking about the nuclear problem. For example, never for a moment would the war planners stop to consider that a lifeline might, in fact, be a more appropriate metaphor than a pendulum. If both superpowers were to see themselves precariously perched on the same lifeline suspended over perilous waters, then each new weapons build-up of either side would only add additional weight to the line, bringing it ever closer to snapping, and in so doing, plunging both sides to their doom.

The fact is, we made a mistake. Our parents made a mistake and so did theirs. It began a long time ago when God said to the first of our kind, "You shall have dominion over the fish of the sea and over the birds of the air and over every living thing that moves upon the earth." We thought God meant for us to subdue the earth, to become its master. So we have spent out lifetimes engaged in battle against the elements. We have fought the rest of the living kingdom. We have locked horns with every living thing in a desperate campaign to gain control, to become sovereign.

We have been very successful. The world has been subdued, and we have become rulers over all things. The statistics tell the grim story of our reign. It is the story of mass genocide: the story of our revenge against the rest of the living kingdom for our having been expelled from the garden.

Our species has become expert executioners. We now can boast of killing off one of God's creatures every sixty minutes. Between now and the year 2000 AD, we will have exterminated nearly 20 percent of all the remaining species left on the planet.

We have misread our mandate. We believed that to have dominion meant to exert power, to control, to dominate. Now, we must ask ourselves to reconsider God's first instruction to our species. Dominion was never meant to be a license to kill. It was never intended as an invitation to rule over the kingdom. When God said, "You shall have dominion," he was calling on us to be a caretaker, a steward of the creation. A steward's role is to preserve, to restore and to heal. Stewards do not exercise power over things. They participate with and nurture other things. Their sense of security does not come from being in control, but rather from taking care of other beings.

How does one begin to assume the role of steward? The first requirement is that life be resacralized at every level of existence. Our parents' generation saw life as profane, an object for manipulation, a factor of production. As a result, life has been reduced to mere statistics, to be targeted on a computer screen in the war-rooms of the world.

It is to be hoped that our generation will rise up in indignation against all efforts to reduce the world to manipulable proportions. Life is not reducible to equations, probability ratios and numbers. Life is not valued as important because it can be productive or profitable or efficient. It is valuable in and of itself. Life is not a means to advance some distant utilitarian end, it is an end. It is not an instrument, it is a gift. Life is not to be judged by what it can do, or accomplish, or how it can be exploited. Instead, all the things we do are to be judged by how well we honor the idea of the sacredness of life.

What a glorious day it would be if our generation were to announce its intentions to march back to the garden armed with a new mandate: a mandate to serve as the stewards of the world, the caretakers of the creation. Would not the gates of Paradise swing open to welcome these new visitors, these bearers of the gift of life, these souls who have consecrated their life to restoring the creation to its rightful place in the universe?

And as our generation walks through those gates, and gazes once again upon the beauty of the garden as Adam and Eve once did, we will be cleansed and rejuvenated. The long, weary journey to secure the immortality of the human race will have ended where it began. Our generation will have finally discovered the sweet secret of immortality.

For time immemorial we have labored under the assumption that our immortality could be secured by building monuments to our own accomplishments. We have stalked the earth, devoured its treasures, surrounded ourselves with the hardware of our own handiwork, convinced that by mastering our environment we could gain a measure of immortality. We could overcome time and space, death and dust by exercising more and more power and control over the forces of nature and each other.

In our desperate search for immortality we have come to see life as an obstacle to overcome. We have used every means at our disposal to fight against the prospect of our own demise. Yet, as history has so well documented, the more frantic our efforts at controlling the life force, the more damage we have inflicted on it.

Our generation has merely to change its perspective regarding the meaning of life and, in so doing, we will have secured the immortality that has so eluded every other generation in history.

Life is not an obstacle to overcome. It is a gift to enjoy. If we experience life as a gift, we give thanks. Giving thanks means sharing our good fortune by helping to extend the gift of life to future generations. We gain a measure of immortality by being a nurturing link in the chain of life. It is by replenishing the rich reservoirs and deep wells that sustain life, and by carefully stewarding the earth that bears and gives forth the fruits of life, that we live on. Our own life force, then, does not die. It is incorporated into every future birth of every living thing that results from our nurturing care. By caring for the creation, we pass on the gift of life, and in the process our spirit is passed on as well. It becomes part of the everlasting continuum that binds together all of the countless gifts of life into a single indivisible web. There can be no greater feeling of security than to become intimately joined to the entire life force of creation.

Our generation has a choice to make: to continue to seek security by travelling the same well worn path that every other generation has headed down over the course of history, only to be disappointed and exhausted at the end of the journey; or to chart a path back to the original garden, to travel home and re-enter the gates of Paradise, determined to begin again, this time as a steward and caretaker of the creation.

Why, we may ask, has our generation been singled out? By what strange quirk of fate have we been handed the responsibility for the life or death of the planet? When one stops to ponder the long history of the human sojourn, the millions upon millions of years in which countless generations have come and gone, adding their small imprint to the collective experience of the human race, the mere thought that our generation will determine whether there will be a future at all is almost too incredible to comprehend.

Some among us will no doubt lament the misfortunes of history that saddled us with the awesome burden of having to save the earth. They will find this great weight of history that has been placed squarely on our generation to be too overwhelming to address. They will feel embittered at all those who came before us for having left us a legacy of such satanic proportions. Yet, like our parents' generations, and their parents' generation, they too will hope to buy time, enough time to pass that legacy on to their children to deal with.

Some among us will live out their life in constant fear, not willing to venture forth and confront the force that threatens their very existence. They will feel imprisoned by their own recalcitrance, condemned to a life sentence of despair and resignation from which they will see no avenue of escape. Every time they hear the screeching of sirens, or glance up into the sky at a foreign object, or are interrupted by a special bulletin on television, their heart will sink, wondering for an interminable moment whether the end is finally at hand. They will always be waiting for that moment when time will have finally run out. When there will be no more. When everything will cease to exist. For these people the future has already been cancelled, because they have psychologically prepared for the extinction of the race.

Life, as we know it, ceases to exist the moment the human mind ceases to contemplate a future. Some among us, then, have already died. While they continue to languish, to listlessly pursue the motions of existence, their spirit has all but been extinguished. The bomb has already taken its toll among some of our generation. It is murdering the spirit, the imagination, the willingness to contemplate a future.

It is to the others among us, who have not yet succumbed to the psychic numbing that is spreading like an epidemic through the race, that we need to make our appeal. We must begin to see ourselves as the chosen ones: the ones who will take on the great task of representing the future of the species; the ones who will represent the interest of all living things on this earth. We must find the stamina that will be required to disarm the world view that has given rise to the bomb. We must not dwell in self-pity or in unnecessary bouts of recrimination which will only sap our strength, making us an easy target for the psychic numbing process that is already immobilizing so many of our peers.

Our generation is very special: it carries the hopes of humanity with it. It is the lightning rod that connects everyone that has ever lived, with everyone that is yet to be. It is to ourselves that we must now look for inspiration and guidance. Our mission is to strike down the illusions that have perpetrated the nuclear syndrome and the Genetic Age and replace them with a new vision of the future. Our generation can serve as the educators of the race, the prophets of a new tomorrow.

There are those who still entertain the illusion that the unthinkable can never happen. We can wean them of their naivete. There are those who sit back and hope that the unthinkable will never happen. We can wrest them from their complacency. There are those who are convinced that the unthinkable is inevitable. We can offer them new hope and purpose.

Our zealous determination to confront the satanic firestorm that lies within us and about us will insure a rebirth of the human spirit, a reawakening of the life force of creation. By looking at the world with different eyes, we will help succeeding generations do the same. By not being afraid to confront long-accepted ways of thinking, we will bring fresh insight and perspective to these troubled times. By not giving in to the plague of defeatism that is now running rampant through the corridors of the culture, we will set a new standard of confidence and resolve which our children can hold on to for support. By reaching out to each other, human being to human being, we will demonstrate that it doesn't take a race of demigods to remake the world anew. After all, it was mortals, of flesh and blood like ourselves, who gave birth to the spirit of the bomb and genetic engineering. It will be mortals, like ourselves, who will now bury that spirit and its deadly instruments. All that is required is a will to do so. That will is already beginning to well up in the bosom of our generation. It is to ourselves then, that we must now look for our salvation. We must become the disarmers of the nuclear and genetic world view and the dispatchers of a new message, a clarion call that can rally the species to the cause of peace.

We must demand our right to a future free of the nuclear nightmare and the vision of a genetically engineered society. But we must also understand that demands alone will not suffice. They only give notice of one's desires. In the final analysis we must be prepared to back-up our demands with an active commitment to a new form of consciousness, one that can erase the need for a nuclear bomb and genetic engineering from the collective consciousness of the human race. But we also must understand that even a change in consciousness is not enough. It only serves notice that one is ready to approach the world in a new and different way.

After all is said and done, we must be willing to act on both our demands and our reborn consciousness. To act, in this regard, is to commit one's life to the preservation of the human race and the preservation of this common globe we inhabit.

Some among us are probably already on the verge of making a commitment, of giving their life over to the struggle to save the human race, but still hesitate out of concern that there might not be enough time left to make a difference. Whether, in fact, there will be enough time depends largely on us. Every act of non-cooperation with the existing world view buys us more time. Every act of conversion to the new empathetic consciousness buys us more time. We make the time by making our peace with the world.

Strange as it may seem, those who have chosen to renounce the old controlling consciousness and who live with an empathetic sensitivity toward their world do not fear the clock. In contrast, those who still live by the old consciousness are always aware of each passing second. For the first group security is ever present. It resides in the simple act of trusting, of being open and vulnerable, of participating in close interrelationship, of being surrounded by a sense of community. For the second group security is always an elusive proposition. It is something just beyond their immediate grasp, for their every present moment is animated by mistrust, paranoia and fear of loss of control.

Those who have embraced an empathetic consciousness do not worry whether there is enough time to win back a measure of security. They are already secure, even in a world knee-deep in nuclear bombs. They remain calm and serene, even as the world becomes more frantic and desperate. For them there is all the time in the world. And it's to them that we must now turn. They will be the leaders of the resistance and the teachers of a new world view.

Somewhere among our generation is the spirit of a Gandhi ready to soar, the spirit of a hundred thousand Martin Luther Kings ready to battle for peace, the spirit of a million Mother Theresas ready to reach out and resacralize the human race. That spirit lies deeply embedded in the soul of each individual and in the soul of the race, only showing itself sparingly in the long history of human affairs. If we have been saving that spirit up for a propitious moment, then certainly now is the time for it to pour forth and anoint our species with the strength it needs to save the world and usher in a new dawn, the eighth day.

Reading List

Reading List

This list is designed to help anyone follow up the ideas suggested in *Declaration of a Heretic*. It is organized under the following headings: "Critique of the Modern World View," "Alternative Philosophies and Epistemologies," "Critical and Empathetic Science," "Imaginative Cognition," "Religion and Spirituality," "Alternative Psychologies," "Holistic Health," "Education for Human Development," "Economics, Politics, Culture and a New World Order," "New Agriculture and Animal Husbandry," "Business and the Workplace," "Ecology and Environmentalism," "Shelter."

Critique of the Modern World View

The following books provide a critical analysis of the scientific, technical, social, cultural, economic and religious values that underlie the modern world view. Also included in this list are books that offer a detailed psychological, epistemological, environmental and anthropological discussion of the impact of the modern world view on human society.

Adams, Henry, *The Degradation of the Democratic Dogma*. New York: Macmillan, 1919.

Barfield, Owen, *History, Guilt and Habit*. Middletown, CT: Wesleyan University Press, 1979.

Barnet, Richard and Muller, Ronald, *Global Reach: The Power of the Multinational Corporations*. New York: Simon & Schuster, 1974.

Barney, Gerald. Director, *The Global 2000 Report to the President*. New York: Penguin, 1981.

Barrett, William, *The Illusion of Technique*. Garden City, NY: Anchor Books, 1979.
Becker, Ernest, *Escape from Evil*. New York: Free Press, 1975.
Bellah, Robert, *The Broken Covenant*. New York: Seabury Press, 1975.
Berger, P. and Luckmann, T., *The Social Construction of Reality*. Garden City, NY: Doubleday, 1972.
Berry, Wendell, *The Unsettling of America: Culture and Agriculture*. New York: Avon Books, 1977.
Brown, Lester, *The Twenty-Ninth Day*. New York: Norton, 1978.
Brown, Norman, *Life Against Death: The Psychoanalytical Meaning of History*. Middletown, CT: Wesleyan University Press, 1959.
Bury, J.B., *The Idea of Progress: An Inquiry into its Origin and Growth*. New York: Dover, 1955.
Butterfield, Herbert, *The Origins of Modern Science*. New York: Free Press, 1965.
Buttel, Frederick and Newby, Howard, eds, *The Rural Sociology of the Advanced Societies: Critical Perspectives*. Montclair, NJ: Allanheld, Osmun & Co., 1980.
Carson, Rachel, *Silent Spring*. Cambridge, MA: The Riverside Press, 1962.
Cavalieri, Liebe, *The Double-Edged Helix: Science in the Real World*. New York: Columbia University Press, 1981.
Chargaff, Erwin, *Voices in the Labyrinth: Nature, Man and Science*. New York: Seabury Press, 1977.
Cornucopia Project, *Empty Breadbasket*. Emmaus, PA: Rodale Press, 1982.
Dahlberg, Kenneth, *Beyond the Green Revolution: The Ecology and Politics of Global Agricultural Development*. New York: Plenum Press, 1979.
Dechert, Charles, ed., *The Social Impact of Cybernetics*. New York: Simon & Schuster, 1967.
Deely, John and Nogar, Raymond, *The Problem of Evolution: A Study of the Philosophical Repercussions of Evolutionary Science*. New York: Appleton-Century-Crofts, 1973.
Diamond, S., *In Search of the Primitive: A Critique of Civilization*. NJ: Rutgers University Press, 1981.
Ehrenfeld, David, *The Arrogance of Humanism*. New York: Oxford, 1978.

Ellul, Jacques, *The Technological Society*. New York: Continuum, 1980.

Ferre, Frederick, *Shaping the Future: Resources for the Post-Modern World*. New York: Harper & Row, 1976.

Feyerabend, Paul, *Against Method: Outline of an Anarchistic Theory of Knowledge*. London: New Left Books, 1975.

Fix, W.R., *The Bone Peddlers: Selling Evolution*. New York: Macmillan, 1984.

Fox, Michael, *Farm Animals: Husbandry, Behavior, and Veterinary Practice*. Baltimore: University Park Press, 1984.

Fromm, Erich, *The Anatomy of Human Destructiveness*. New York: Fawcett, 1973.

Gellner, Ernest, *Legitimation of Belief*. London: Cambridge University Press, 1974.

Giarini, Orio and Louberge, Henri, *The Diminishing Returns of Technology*. Oxford: Pergamon Press, 1978.

Gray, Elizabeth, *Green Paradise Lost*. Wellesly, MA: Roundtable Press, 1982.

Guénon, René, *The Reign of Quantity and The Signs of the Times*. Baltimore: Penguin Books, 1953.

Gurvitch, Georges, *The Social Frameworks of Knowledge*. Oxford: Basil Blackwell, 1971.

Habermas, Jurgen, *Knowledge and Human Interest*. Boston: Beacon Press, 1971.

——, *Legitimation Crisis*. Boston: Beacon Press, 1975.

Hayes, Carlton, *Nationalism: A Religion*. New York: Macmillan, 1960.

Heidegger, Martin, *The Question Concerning Technology*. New York: Harper & Row, 1977.

Heilbroner, Robert, *An Inquiry into the Human Prospect*. New York: Norton, 1974.

Hillman, James, *The Myth of Analysis: Three Essays in Archetypal Psychology*. New York: Harper & Row, 1972.

Hirsch, Fred, *Social Limits to Growth*, Cambridge, MA: Harvard University Press, 1978.

Hitching, Francis, *The Neck of the Giraffe: Where Darwin Went Wrong*. New York: Holt, Rinehart & Winston, 1982.

Hoos, Ida, *Systems Analysis in Public Policy*. Berkely: University of California Press, 1972.

Horkheimer, Max and Adorno, Theodor, *Dialectic of Enlighten-*

ment. New York: Herder & Herder, 1972.
Howard, Ted and Rifkin, Jeremy, *Who Should Play God?* New York: Dell Publishing Co., 1977.
Illich, Ivan, *Medical Nemesis*. New York: Bantam, 1977.
Jaki, Stanley L., *Angels, Apes and Men*. La Salle, IL: Sherwood Sugden, 1983.
Koestler, Arthur and Smythies, James, *Beyond Reductionism*. New York: Macmillan, 1970.
Kuhn, Thomas, *The Structure of Scientific Revolutions*, 2nd ed. University of Chicago Press, 1970.
Kohr, Leopold, *Development without Aid: The Translucent Society*. Llandybie, Wales: Christopher Davies, 1973.
——, *The Overdeveloped Nations: The Diseconomies of Scale*. Schocken, 1977.
Lasch, Christopher, *The Culture of Narcissism: American Life in an Age of Diminishing Expectations*. New York: Norton, 1978.
——, *Haven in a Heartless World: The Family Besieged*. New York: Basic Books, 1977.
Levinas, Emmanuel, *Totality and Infinity*. Pittsburgh: Duquesne University Press, 1969.
Lewis, C.S., *The Abolition of Man*. New York: Macmillan, 1947.
Macbeth, Norman, *Darwin Retried: An Appeal to Reason*. Boston: Gambit, 1971.
Marcuse, Herbert, *One Dimensional Man*. Boston: Beacon Press, 1964.
Mayraeder, Rosa, *A Survey of the Woman Problem*. CT: Hyperion, 1981.
McLuhan, Marshall, *The Gutenberg Galaxy*. New York: Mentor Books, 1969.
——, *The Medium is the Message*. New York: Bantam Books, 1967.
Meadows, Donella, Meadows, Dennis, et. al., *The Limits to Growth*. Washington: DC: Potomac Associates, 1972.
Merchant, Carolyn, *The Death of Nature: Women, Ecology and the Scientific Revolution*. San Francisco: Harper & Row, 1980.
Miles, Ian and Irvine, John, eds, *The Poverty of Progress*. Oxford: Pergamon Press, 1982.
Mishran, Ezra, *The Costs of Economic Growth*. New York: Praeger, 1969.
——, *The Economic Growth Debate*. London: Allen & Unwin, 1977.
Mitcham, Carl and Mackey, Robert, eds, *Philosophy and*

Technology: Readings in the Philosophical Problems of Technology. New York: Free Press, 1972.

Moorhead, Paul and Kaplan, Martin, eds, *Mathematical Challenges to the Neo-Darwinian Interpretation of Evolution*. Philadelphia: Wistar Institute Press, 1967.

Mumford, Lewis, *Technics and Civilization*. New York: Harcourt Brace Jovanovich, 1934.

——, *The Myth of the Machine: Technics and Human Development*. New York: Harcourt Brace Jovanovich, 1966.

Mulkay, Michael, *Science and the Sociology of Knowledge*. London: Allen & Unwin, 1979.

Oakley, Francis, *The Medieval Experience: Foundations of Western Cultural Singularity*. New York: Scribner's, 1974.

Ravetz, Jerome, *Scientific Knowledge and Its Social Problems*. New York: Oxford University Press, 1973.

Rifkin, Jeremy with Howard, Ted, *Entropy: A New World View*, New York: Viking, 1980.

——, *The Emerging Order: God in the Age of Scarcity*. New York: Ballantine, 1983.

Rifkin, Jeremy in collaboration with Perlas, Nicanor, *Algeny*. New York: Viking, 1983.

Roszak, Theodore, *Where the Wasteland Ends: Politics and Transcendence in Post-Industrial Society*. Garden City, NY: Anchor/Doubleday, 1973.

Sahlins, Marshall, *The Use and Abuse of Biology: An Anthropological Critique of Sociobiology*. Ann Arbor: University of Michigan Press, 1976.

Schrödinger, Erwin, *What is Life? The Physical Aspect of the Living Cell*. New York: Macmillan, 1947.

Shepard, Paul, *Nature and Madness*. San Francisco: Sierra Club Books, 1982.

Slater, Philip, *The Pursuit of Loneliness*. Boston: Beacon, 1976.

Spengler, Oswald, *The Decline of the West*, Vol. 1. New York: Knopf, 1926.

Steiner, Rudolf, *The Boundaries of Natural Science*. Spring Valley, NY: Anthroposophic Press, 1983.

Stent, Gunther, *Paradoxes of Progress*, San Francisco: W.H. Freeman, 1978.

Teich, Albert, ed., *Technology and Man's Future*. New York: St. Martin's Press, 1972.

Thompson, William, *At the Edge of History*. New York: Harper & Row, 1971.
Turkle, Sherry, *The Second Self: Computers and the Human Spirit*. New York: Simon & Schuster, 1984.
Waddington, Conrad, *The Evolution of an Evolutionist*. Edinburgh University Press, 1975.
Weizenbaum, Joseph, *Computer Power and Human Reason: From Judgement to Calculation*. San Francisco: W.H. Freeman, 1976.
Whitehead, Alfred North, *Science and the Modern World*. New York: Macmillan, 1925.
Wilkinson, Richard, *Poverty and Progress*. New York: Praeger, 1973.
Winner, Langdon, *Autonomous Technology*. Cambridge, MA: MIT Press, 1977.

Alternative Philosophies and Epistemologies

The books in this category explore new approaches to consciousness and knowledge, with emphasis on developing an empathetic and participatory union between the human mind and nature.

Barfield, Owen, *Saving the Appearances: A Study in Idolatry*. New York: Harcourt Brace Jovanovich, 1965.
Bebek, Borna, *The Third City: Philosophy at War with Positivism*. London: Routledge & Kegan Paul, 1982.
Berman, Morris, *The Reenchantment of the World*. Ithaca, NY: Cornell University Press, 1981.
Campbell, Joseph, *Hero with a Thousand Faces*. New York: Meridian, 1956.
Cassirer, Ernst, *The Philosophy of Symbolic Forms*, 3 vols. New Haven, CT: Yale University Press, 1953-1957.
Comfort, Alex, *Reality and Empathy*. Albany: State University of New York, 1984.
Deloria, Vine, Jr., *The Metaphysics of Modern Existence*. San Francisco: Harper & Row, 1979.
Fraser, J.T., *Of Time, Passion, and Knowledge*. New York: George Braziller, 1975.
——, *The Voices of Time*. Amherst: University of Massachusetts Press, 1981.

——, et. al., *The Study of Time*, 4 vols. Berlin/Heidelberg: Springer-Verlag, 1972-1981.

Gadamer, Hans-Georg, *Truth and Method*. New York: Crossroad, 1975.

Gilson, Etienne, *From Aristotle to Darwin and Back Again*. University of Notre Dame Press, 1984.

Glacken, Clarence, *Traces on the Rhodian Shore*. Berkeley and Los Angeles: University of California Press, 1967.

Gurevich, A.J., *Categories of Medieval Culture*. London: Routledge & Kegan Paul, 1985.

Hallpike, C.R., *The Foundations of Primitive Thought*. Oxford: Clarendon Press, 1979.

Herbert, Nick, *Quantum Reality*. London: Rider, 1985.

Jantsch, E. and Waddington, C. eds, *Evolution and Consciousness*. Reading, MA: Addison-Wesley, 1976.

Jaynes, Julian, *The Origin of Consciousness in the Breakdown of the Bicameral Mind*. Boston: Houghton Mifflin, 1976.

Kaufmann, Walter, *Discovering the Mind: Goethe, Kant and Hegel*. New York: McGraw-Hill, 1980.

Kohak, Erazim, *The Embers and the Stars: A Philosophical Inquiry into the Moral Sense of Nature*. University of Chicago Press, 1984.

Kuhlewind, Georg, *Stages of Consciousness*. MA: Lindisfarne Press, 1984.

Langer, Susanne, *Feeling and Form: A Theory of Art*. New York: Charles Scribner's Sons, 1953.

——, *Mind: An Essay on Human Feeling*, 2 vols. Baltimore and London: Johns Hopkins Press, 1967, 1972.

Lonergan, Bernard, *Insight*. New York: Harper & Row, 1978.

MacIntyre, Alastair, *After Virtue*. University of Notre Dame Press, 1981.

Margenau, Henry and Sellon, Emily, eds, *Nature, Man, and Society: Main Currents in Modern Thought*. York Beach, ME: Nicolas-Hays, 1976.

Maturana, Humberto and Varela, Francisco, *Autopoesis and Cognition*. Dordrecht, Netherlands: Reidel, 1979.

Neuman, Erich, *The Origins and History of Consciousness*. New York: Pantheon Books, 1954.

Ong, Walter, *Interfaces of the Word: Studies in the Evolution of Consciousness and Culture*. Ithaca: Cornell University Press, 1977.

Polak, Fred, *The Image of the Future*, Vol. 1. Leyden, Netherlands: A.W. Sijthoff, 1961.
Rollin, Bernard, *Animal Rights*. Buffalo, NY: Prometheus Books, 1981.
Shallis, Michael, *On Time*. Schocken, 1983.
Slater, Philip, *The Wayward Gate: Science and the Supernatural*. Boston: Beacon Press, 1977.
Spencer-Brown, George, *Laws of Form*. New York: Bantam, 1973.
Walker, Stephen, *Animal Thought*. London: Routledge & Kegan Paul, 1983.
Weizsacker, Carl Friedrich von, *The Unity of Nature*. New York: Farrar, Straus & Giroux, 1980.
West, John Anthony, *Serpent in the Sky*. New York: Harper & Row, 1979.
Wilber, Ken, *Up From Eden: A Transpersonal View of Human Evolution*. Boulder, CO: Shambhala, 1983.
Yates, Frances, *Giordano Bruno and the Heremetic Tradition*. London: Routledge & Kegan Paul, 1964.
Young, Arthur, *The Bell Notes: A Journey from Physics to Metaphysics*. New York: Delacorte Press/Seymour Lawrence, 1979.
——, *The Reflexive Universe*. New York: Delacorte Press/Seymour Lawrence, 1976.

Critical and Empathetic Science

These books offer a contrasting vision to Baconian science. In place of the traditional scientific method which emphasizes objective detachment and power over the forces of nature, these authors concentrate on developing an empathetic methodology in which the knowledge of relationship is the primary focus.

Bateson, Gregory, *Mind and Nature: A Necessary Unity*. New York: E.P. Dutton, 1979.
Brokensha, D.W., Warren, D.M. and Werner, O., eds, *Indigenous Knowledge Systems and Development*. Lanham, MD: University Press of America, 1980.
Burr, Harold Saxton, *Blueprint for Immortality: The Electric*

Patterns of Life. London: Neville Spearman, 1972.

Cobb, John, Jr. and Griffin, David, *Mind in Nature: Essays on the Interface of Science and Philosophy*. Washington DC: University Press of America, 1977.

Collingwood, R.G., *The Idea of Nature*. Oxford University Press, 1945.

Devall, Bill and Sessions, George, *Deep Ecology*. Salt Lake City, UT: Peregrine Smith Books, 1985.

Goethe, J.W. von, *The Metamorphosis of Plants*. Wyoming, RI: Bio-Dynamic Literature, 1978.

Grasse, Pierre-P., *Evolution of Living Organisms: Evidence for a New Theory of Transformation*. New York: Academic Press, 1977.

Haraway, Donna Jeanne, *Crystals, Fabrics, and Fields: Metaphors of Organism in Twentieth-Century Developmental Biology*. New Haven: Yale University Press, 1976.

Jantsch, Erich, *The Self-Organizing Universe*. Oxford: Pergamon Press, 1980.

Jones, Roger, *Physics as Metaphor*. New York: New American Library, 1982.

Lovelock, J.E., *Gaia: A New Look at Life on Earth*. Oxford University Press, 1979.

Lovtrup, Soren, *Epigenetics: A Treatise on Theoretical Biology*. London: John Wiley, n.d.

Pedler, Kit, *The Quest for Gaia*. London: Granada, 1981.

Pitman, Michael, *Adam and Evolutin*. London: Rider, 1984.

Schwenk, Theodor, *Sensitive Chaos: The Creation of Flowing Forms in Water and Air*. London: Rudolf Steiner Press, 1965.

Sheldrake, Rupert, *A New Science of Life*. Los Angeles: J.P. Tarcher, 1981.

Sperry, Roger, *Science and Moral Priority*. New York: Columbia University Press, 1983.

Tomlin, E.W.F., *Psyche, Culture and the New Science*. London: Routledge & Kegan Paul, 1985.

Varela, Francisco, *Principles of Biological Autonomy*. Amsterdam: North Holland, 1979.

Weiss, Paul, *The Science of Life: The Living System – A System for Living*. New York: Futura, 1973.

Wilber, Ken, ed., *The Holographic Paradigm and Other Paradoxes*. Boulder, CO: Shambhala, 1982.

Imaginative Cognition

These books delve into human thought processes in entirely new ways. An increasing number of scholars have begun to examine the mind as an imaginative, creative medium. This new approach to the mind offers a rather interesting contrast to traditional studies on consciousness, which have long focused on the mind as a processing receptor for the absorption of external stimulus and information. In these books, consciousness is looked at as an initiating forum as opposed to just a screening device.

Abrams, M.H., *Natural Supernaturalism: The Tradition and Revolution in Romantic Literature*. New York: Norton, 1971.

Avens, Roberts, *Imagination is Reality*. Dallas, TX: Spring Publications, 1980.

Barfield, Owen, *Poetic Diction: A Study in Meaning*. Middletown, CT: Wesleyan University Press, 1973.

——, *The Rediscovery of Meaning, and Other Essays*. Middletown, CT: Wesleyan University Press, 1977.

Bohm, David, *Wholeness and the Implicate Order*. London: Routledge & Kegan Paul, 1980.

Hayward, Jeremy, *Perceiving Ordinary Magic: Science and Intuitive Wisdom*. Boulder, CO: Shambhala, 1984.

Holton, Gerald, *The Scientific Imagination: Case Studies*. New York: Cambridge University Press, 1978.

Lakoff, George and Johnson, Marle, eds, *Metaphors We Live By*. University of Chicago Press, 1980.

Levere, Trevor, *Poetry Realized in Nature: Samuel Taylor Coleridge and Early Nineteenth-Century Science*. Cambridge University Press, 1981.

Polanyi, Michael, *Personal Knowledge: Towards a Post-Critical Philosophy*. University of Chicago Press, 1962.

Ricoeur, Paul, *The Rule of Metaphor*. University of Toronto Press, 1977.

Rothenberg, Albert, *The Emerging Goddess: The Creative Process in Art Science, and Other Fields*. University of Chicago Press, 1979.

Sloan, Douglas, *Insight-Imagination: The Emancipation of Thought and the Modern World*. Westport, CT: Greenwood Press, 1983.

Sugarman, Shirley, ed., *Evolution of Consciousness: Studies in Polarity*. Middletown, CT: Wesleyan University Press, 1976.
Taylor, A.M., *Imagination and the Growth of Science*. New York: Schocken Books, 1970.
Warnock, Mary, *Imagination*. Berkeley and Los Angeles: University of California Press, 1976.
Wheelwright, Philip, *Metaphor and Reality*. Bloomington: Indiana University Press, 1962.

Religion and Spirituality

These books focus on the changing interpretation of Judaeo-Christian theology that has accompanied the new ecological awareness. The starting point for discussion in most of these books is the redefinition of dominion as stewardship rather than subjugation of nature. References in the Old Testament to humanity's relationship to the land, environment and creation is given new meaning in light of the current interest in protecting the earth's ecosystems. New Testament theology centers on Christ and the Crucifixion as the archetypal empathetic experience.

Other books deal more generally with the development of a new spirituality that is compatible (congenial) with the new consciousness, the new science and the new ecological understanding.

Religion

Berry, Thomas, *Teilhard in the Ecological Age*. Chambersburg, PA: Anima Books, 1982.
Carmody, John, *Ecology and Religion: Toward a New Christian Theology of Nature*. Ramsey, NJ: Paulist Press, 1983.
Derrick, C., *The Delicate Creation: Towards a Theology of the Environment*. Old Greenwich, CT: Devin-Adair, 1972.
Michaelson, Wesly Granberg-, *A Worldly Spirituality: The Call to Redeem Life on Earth*. New York: Harper & Row, 1984.
Norman, Edward, *Christianity and the World Order*. New York: Oxford University Press, 1979.
Rifkin, Jeremy with Howard, Ted, *The Emerging Order*. New York: Ballatine Books, 1983.
Schaeffer, Francis, *Pollution and the Death of Man: The Christian*

View of Ecology. Wheaton, IL: Tyndale House, 1970.
Wilkinson, Loren, *Earthkeeping: Christian Stewardship of National Resources*. Grand Rapids, MI: William B. Erdmans, 1980.

Spirituality

Bentov, Itzhak, *Stalking the Wild Pendulum: On the Mechanics of Consciousness*. New York: Bantam Books, 1977.
Berger, Peter, *The Sacred Canopy*. Garden City, NY: Doubleday, 1967.
Boyd, Doug, *Rolling Thunder*. New York: Delta, 1974.
Brandon, S.G.F., *History, Time and Deity*. New York: Manchester University Press/Barnes & Noble, 1965.
Brown, Joseph Epes, *The Spiritual Legacy of the American Indian*. New York: Crossroad, 1982.
Bucke, M., *Cosmic Consciousness*. New York: Dutton, 1923.
Eliade, Mircea, *The Myth of the Eternal Return*. Princeton University Press, 1954.
Huxley, Aldous, *The Perennial Philosophy*. New York: Harper & Row, 1970.
Kapleau, P., *The Three Pillars of Zen*. Boston: Beacon, 1965.
Leonard, George, *The Silent Pulse*. New York: E.P. Dutton, 1978.
Merleau-Ponty, Jacques and Morando, Bruno, *The Rebirth of Cosmology*. New York: Alfred A. Knopf, 1976.
Miller, David, *The New Polytheism: Rebirth of Gods and Goddesses*. New York: Harper & Row, 1974.
Nasr, Seyyed Hossein, *Knowledge and the Sacred*. Gifford Lectures, 1981. New York: Crossroad, 1981.
Needleman, Jacob, *A Sense of the Cosmos: The Encounter of Ancient Wisdom and Modern Science*. Garden City, NY: Doubleday, 1975.
Peck, M. Scott, *The Road Less Traveled*. Oregon: Touchstone Books, 1980.
Schumacher, E.F., *A Guide for the Perplexed*. New York: Harper & Row, 1977.
Shepherd, A.P., *Scientist of the Invisible: Spiritual Science, The Life and Work of Rudolf Steiner*. New York: Inner Traditions, 1984.
Smith, Huston, *Beyond the Post-Modern Mind*. New York: Crossroad, 1982.
Spangler, David, *Revelation: The Birth of a New Age*, 2nd ed. San

Francisco: Rainbow Bridge, 1976.
Teilhard de Chardin, P., *The Phenomenon of Man*. New York: Harper & Row, 1964.
Suzuki, D.T., *An Introduction to Zen Buddhism*. New York: Grove, 1964.

Alternative Psychologies

These books go beyond the mechanistic framework of orthodox psychology by establishing a more integrative conception in which psyche and environment become meshed in a single, multi-dimensional whole. In place of the old idea of consciousness as an independent, isolated phenomena, the new theories of psychology place greater emphasis on consciousness as immanent, all-pervasive and permeating every level of existence.

Many of these books go well beyond the older forms of reductionist psychology, to examine the individual as a temporal, spiritual, and ethical being.

Assagioli, Roberto, *Psychosynthesis*. New York: Viking, 1971.
Buber, Martin, *I and Thou*. New York: Scribner's, 1958.
Eccles, John, *The Human Mystery*. Gifford Lectures, 1978. London: Routledge & Kegan Paul, 1984.
Frankl, Viktor, *Unheard Cry for Meaning: Psychotherapy and Humanism*. New York: Simon & Schuster, 1978.
Hampden-Turner, Charles, *Maps of the Mind: Charts and Concepts of the Mind and Its Labyrinths*. New York: Macmillan, 1981.
Heard, Gerald, *The Five Ages of Man: The Psychology of Human History*. New York: Julian Press, 1963.
Hillman, James, *Re-Visioning Psychology*. New York: Harper & Row, 1975.
Hooper, Judith and Teresi, Dick, *Cartographers of Consciousness*. London: Rider, 1985.
Jung, Carl, *The Archetypes and the Collective Unconscious*. Princeton University Press, 1969.
——, *Memories, Dreams and Reflections*. New York: Vintage, 1961.
——, *Structure and Dynamics of the Psyche*. Collected Works, Vol.

8. Princeton University Press, 1968.
Kohler, W., *Gestalt Psychology*. New York: Liverwright, 1929.
Leonard, George, *The Transformation: A Guide to the Inevitable Changes in Humankind*. New York: Delta, 1972.
LeShan, Lawrence, *Alternate Realities: The Search for the Full Human Being*. New York: Ballantine, 1976.
Levin, David Michael, *The Body's Recollection of Being: Phenomenological Psychology and the Deconstruction of Nihilism*. London: Routledge & Kegan Paul, 1985.
Lowenthal, David and Bowden, Martyn, eds, *Geographies of the Mind*. Oxford University Press, 1976.
Maslow, Abraham, *Toward a Psychology of Being*. New York: Van Nostrand Reinhold, 1968.
——, *Motivation and Personality*. New York: Harper & Row, 1970.
——, *The Farther Reaches of Human Nature*. New York: Viking, 1971.
May, Rollo, *Man's Search for Himself*. New York: Delta, 1953.
——, *Love and Will*. New York: Norton, 1969.
Miller, Jean, *Toward a New Psychology of Women*. Boston: Beacon, 1976.
Mitchell, Edgar and White, John, eds, *Psychic Exploration: A Challenge for Science*, Capricorn, 1974.
Ouspensky, P.D., *The Psychology of Man's Possible Evolution*. New York: Random, 1973.
——, *Tertium Organum: A Key to the Enigmas of the World*. New York: Random, 1981.
Ornstein, Robert, *The Psychology of Consciousness*. New York: Viking, 1973.
Popper, Karl and Eccles, John, *The Self and Its Brain: An Argument for Interactionism*. New York: Springer International, 1977.
Rank, Otto, *Beyond Psychology*. New York: Dover, 1941.
Rogers, Carl, *On Becoming a Person: A Therapist's View of Psychotherapy*. Houghton Mifflin, 1961.
Scheler, Max, *Man's Place in Nature*. New York: Farrar, Straus & Giroux, 1961.
Solovyev, Vladimir, *The Meaning of Love*. New York: International Universities Press, n.d.
Steiner, Rudolf, *The Case for Anthroposophy*. Spring Valley, NY:

Anthroposophic Press, 1970.
Snyder, Gary, *The Real Work: Interviews and Talks: 1964-1979*. New York: New Directions, 1980.
Tart, Charles, ed., *Transpersonal Psychologies*. New York: Harper & Row, 1975.
Trungpa, C., *Cutting Through Spiritual Materialism*. Boulder, CO: Shambhala, 1973.
Wilber, Ken, *The Atman Project*. Wheaton, IL: Theosophical Publishing Co., 1980.

Holistic Health

These books emphasize "wellness" over sickness, and prevention over cure. In this new approach to medicine, attention is placed not on isolating illnesses but rather on understanding the overall physiological, psychological and spiritual context which gives rise to specific diseases. Basic environmental considerations that are often ignored in the diagnosis and treatment of illness are given a renewed importance – including nutrition, sanitation and hygiene. The healing process relies more on the natural restorative rhythms.

Cohen, John, *Psychological Time in Health and Disease*, Charles C. Thomas, 1967.
Conry, Barbara, *An Existential-Phenomenological View of the Lived Body*. PhD Dissertation. Ohio State University, 1974.
Dossey, Larry, *Space, Time, and Medicine*. Boulder, CO: Shambhala, 1982.
——, *Beyond Illness: Discovering the Experience of Health*. Boulder, CO: Shambhala, 1984.
Hastings, Arthur, Fadiman, James and Gordon, James, eds, *Health for the Whole Person*. Boulder, CO: Westview Press, 1980.
Mattson, Phyllis. *Holistic Health in Perspective*. Palo Alto, CA: Mayfield, 1982.
Pelletier, Kenneth, *Holistic Medicine*. New York: Dell, 1980.
Popenoe, Cris, ed., *Wellness*. New York: Random, 1977.
Schaefer, K.E., Hensel, H., and Brady, R., eds, *Toward a Man-Centered Medical Science*. Mt Kisco, New York: Futura Publishing Co., 1977.

Straus, Erwin, *The Primary World of Senses*. Glencoe, New York: Free Press of Glencoe, 1963.
Tournier, Paul, *The Medicine of the Whole Person*. Word Books, 1973.
——, *Creative Suffering*. New York: Harper & Row, 1983.
Zaner, R., *The Context of Self*. Athens: Ohio University Press, 1981.

Education for Human Development

These books explore the limits of an overly utilitarian approach to education. Humankind is more than a tool to be fashioned to serve the interests of industry and the state. Appropriate education nurtures the whole person and sensitively guides individuals to be free and creative actors in life.

Arons, Stephen, *Compelling Belief: The Culture of American Schooling*. New York: McGraw-Hill, 1983.
Bettelheim, Bruno, *The Uses of Enchantment: The Meaning and Importance of Fairy Tales*. New York: Knopf, 1977.
Cobb, Edith, *The Ecology of Imagination in Childhood*. New York: Columbia University Press, 1977.
Chall, Jeanne and Mirski, Allan, eds, *Education and the Brain*. University of Chicago Press, 1978.
Gruber, H. and Vonèche, J., eds, *The Essential Piaget*. New York: Basic Books, 1977.
Harwood, A.C., *The Recovery of Man in Childhood: A Study in the Educational Work of Rudolf Steiner*. London: Hodder & Stoughton, 1958.
Holt, John, *Escape from Childhood: The Needs and Rights of Children*. New York: Ballantine, 1974.
——, *Instead of Education: Ways to Help People Do Things Better*. New York: Delta, 1976.
Kozol, J., *Death at an Early Age*. New York: Bantam, 1970.
——, *On Being a Teacher*. New York: Continuum, 1981.
Lerner, Max, *Values in Education: Notes Towards a Values Philosophy*. Phi Delta Kappa, 1976.
Pearce, Joseph, *The Crack in the Cosmic Egg*. New York: Julian Press, 1971.
Piaget, Jean, *The Child's Conception of Time*. New York: Basic Books, 1969.

Sloan, Douglas, ed., *Education and Values*. New York: Teachers College Press, 1980.

Economics, Politics, Culture and a New World Order

This list of books surveys revolutionary new approaches to the organization of society. Several popular themes are woven into each of these broad subject areas. These include a renewed sense of the idea of community, the interdependency and mutuality of all political, economic and cultural relationships and an emphasis on the concept of indebtedness as both an ethical value and an environmental rule. Many of the books center on the ecological context which circumscribes all social endeavors.

The authors in this list approach their subject areas with a new orientation. The traditional objective methodology of observation, analysis and intervention is replaced by a perspective methodology, that emphasizes empathy and participation as a means of reimagining and remaking the social experience.

Berdyaev, Nikolai, *Slavery and Freedom*. NY: Scribner's, 1944.

Berger, Peter, Berger, B. and Kellner, H., *The Homeless Mind: Modernization and Consciousness*. New York: Vintage, 1973.

Birch, Charles and Cobb, John, *The Liberation of Life: From the Cell to the Community*. Cambridge University Press, 1983.

Bookchin, Murray, *The Ecology of Freedom: The Emergence and Dissolution of Hierarchy*. Palo Alto, CA: Cheshire Books, 1982.

Brown, Lester, *Building a Sustainable Society*. NY: Norton, 1981.

Callenbach, Ernest, *Ecotopia*. New York: Bantam Books, 1977.

Capra, Fritjof and Spretnak, Charlene, *The Turning Point*. New York: Simon & Schuster, 1982.

——, *Green Politics: The Global Promise*. New York: Dutton, 1984.

Cottle, J.T. and Klineberg, S., *The Present of Things Future*. New York: Free Press, 1974.

Daly, Herman, *Steady-State Economics: The Economics of Biophysical Equilibrium and Moral Growth*. San Francisco: W.H. Freeman, 1977.

Daly, Mary, *Beyond God the Father: Toward a Philosophy of Women's Liberation*. Boston: Beacon, 1973.

Davy, Charles, *Towards a Third Culture*. London: Faber & Faber, 1961.

Doob, Leonard, *Patterning of Time*. New Haven, CT: Yale University Press, 1971.

Doxiadis, Constantinos, *Anthropopolis: City for Human Development*. New York: Norton, 1974.

Durbin, Paul, *A Guide to the Culture of Science, Technology, and Medicine*. New York: Free Press, 1980.

Elgin, Duane, *Voluntary Simplicity: Toward a Way of Life that is Outwardly Simple, Inwardly Rich*. New York: Morrow, 1981.

Ferkiss, Victor, *The Future of Technological Civilization*, NY: Braziller, 1974.

Friedmann, John, *Retracking America: A Theory of Transactive Planning*. New York: Anchor, 1973.

George, Henry, *Poverty and Progress*. New York: Robert Schalkenbach Foundation, 1962.

Georgescu-Roegen, Nicholas, *The Entropy Law and the Economic Process*. Cambridge, MA: Harvard University Press, 1971.

——, *Energy and Economic Myths*. Elmsford, NY: Pergamon Press, 1977.

——, *The Entropy Law and the Economic Process*. Cambridge, MA: Harvard University Press, 1971.

Hall, Edward T., *The Dance of Life: The Other Dimension of Time*. New York: Anchor Press/Doubleday, 1983.

Harman, Willis, *An Incomplete Guide to the Future*. San Francisco Book Co., 1976.

Hawken, Paul, *The Next Economy*. New York: Holt, Rinehart & Winston, 1983.

Henderson, Hazel, *Creating Alternative Futures*. New York: Berkley Winhover, 1978.

——, *Politics of the Solar Age: The Alternative to Economics*. New York: Doubleday, 1981.

Katz, Michael et al., eds, *Earth's Answer: Explorations of Planetary Culture at the Lindisfarne Conferences*. New York: Harper & Row, 1977.

Keys, Donald, *Earth at Omega: Passage to Planetization*. Boston: Brandon Press, 1982.

Kohr, Leopold, *The Breakdown of Nations*. Llandybie, Wales: Christopher Davies, 1957.

Large, Martin, *Social Ecology*. Gloucester, England: M.H. Large, 1981.

Lee, Dorothy, *Freedom and Culture*. New Jersey: Prentice Hall, 1959.

Lipnack, Jessica and Stamps, Jeffrey, *Networking: The First Directory*.

Macy, Joanna, *Dharma and Development*. Hartford, CT: Kumarian Press, 1983.

McLuhan, Marshall, *Understanding Media: The Extensions of Man*. New York: McGraw-Hill, 1964.

Mendelovitz, Saul, ed., *On the Creation of a Just World Order: Preferred Worlds for the 1990s*. New York: Free Press, 1975.

Millman, Marcia and Kanter Rosabeth, eds, *Another Voice: Feminist Perspectives on Social Life and Social Science*. New York: Anchor, 1975.

Mische, Gerald and Mische, Patricia, *Toward a Human World Order: Beyond the National Security Jacket*. Ramsey, NJ: Paulist Press, 1977.

Ogilvy, James, *Many Dimensional Man: Decentralizing Self, Society, and the Sacred*. New York: Harper & Row, 1979.

Ophuls, William, *Ecology and the Politics of Scarcity*. San Francisco: W.H. Freeman, 1977.

Rifkin, Jeremy with Howard, Ted, *Entropy: A New World View*. New York: Viking, 1980.

Roheim, Geza, *Psychoanalysis and Anthropology: Culture, Personality and the Unconscious*. New York: International Universities Press, 1968.

Roszak, Theodore, *Person/Planet: The Creative Disintegration of Industrial Society*. New York: Anchor, 1978.

Satin, Mark, *New Age Politics: Healing Self and Society*. New York: Dell, 1978.

Schumacher, E.F., *Small is Beautiful*. New York: Harper & Row, 1973.

Sharp, Gene, *The Politics of Nonviolent Action*. Boston: Porter Sargent, 1973.

Sorokin, P., *Social and Cultural Dynamics*, 4 vols. New York: Bedminster Press, 1962.

Spretnak, Charlene, *The Politics of Women's Spirituality*. New York: Doubleday, 1982.

Stokes, Bruce, *Helping Ourselves*. New York: Norton, 1981.

Thompson, William, *Passages About Earth*. New York: Harper & Row, 1974.

Wilken, Folkert, *The Liberation of Capital*. London: Allen & Unwin, 1982.

New Agriculture and Animal Husbandry

These books approach agriculture and animal husbandry from a redefined perspective regarding the nature of productivity. In the new agriculture, productivity is defined less in terms of efficiency and more in terms of duration. Agricultural resources are seen as an endowment to be stewarded. Agricultural policy is based on the principle of providing not only for the present generation but also for future generations as well. The land and the germplasm is regarded as a sacred trust to be used in a manner that reflects a deep respect for the life process.

Altieri, Miguel, *Agroecology: The Scientific Basis of Alternative Agriculture*. Berkeley, CA: Division of Biological Control, University of California, 1984.

Besson, Jean-Marc and Vogtmann, Hardy, eds, *Towards a Sustainable Agriculture*. Switzerland: Verlag Wirz Aarau, 1978.

Douglas, Gordon, ed., *Agricultural Sustainability in a Changing World Order*. Boulder, CO: Westview Press, 1984.

Douglas, J.S. and Hard, R., *Forest Farming: Towards a Solution to Problems of World Hunger and Conservation*. London: Watkins, 1976.

Findhorn Community, *The Findhorn Garden*. New York: Harper & Row, 1975.

Fox, Michael, *Farm Animals: Husbandry, Behavior, and Veterinary Practice*. Baltimore: University Park Press, 1984.

Fukuoka, M., *One Straw Revolution: An Introduction to Natural Farming*. Emmaus, PA: Rodale Press, 1978.

Harwood, Richard, *Small Farm Development: Understanding and Improving Farming Systems in the Humid Tropics*. Boulder, CO: Westview Press, 1979.

House, G.J., Stinner, B.R. and Lawrence, R., eds, *Agriculture Ecosystems: Unifying Concepts*. New York: John Wiley, In Press.

Jackson, Wes, *New Roots for Agriculture*. San Francisco: Friends of the Earth, 1980.

Jeavons, John, *How to Grow More Vegetables*. CA: Ten Speed Press, 1983.

Kass, D.C., *Polyculture Cropping Systems: Review and Analysis*. Ithaca, New York: Cornell International Agriculture Bulletin, No. 32, 1978.

King, F.H., *Farmers of Forty Centuries*. London: Cape, 1927.

Kolisko, E. and Kolisko, L., *Agriculture of Tomorrow*. Bournemouth, England: Kolisko Archive Publications, 1978.

Lockeretz, W., ed., *Environmentally Sound Agriculture*. New York: Praeger, 1983.

Merrill, Richard, *Radical Agriculture*. New York: Harper & Row, 1976.

Mollison, B., *Permaculture: Practical Design for Town and Country in Permanent Agriculture*. Victoria, Australia: Tagari Books, 1979.

Oelhaf, R.C., *Organic Agriculture*. Montclair, NJ: Allanheld, Osmun & Co., 1978.

Regan, Tom, *The Case for Animal Rights*. London: Routledge & Kegan Paul, 1983.

Smith, J.R., *Tree Crops: A Permanent Agriculture*. New York: Devin-Adair, 1953.

Stonehouse, B., ed., *Biological Husbandry: A Scientific Approach to Organic Farming*. London: Butterworth, 1981.

Tilth, *The Future is Abundant: A Guide to Sustainable Agriculture*. Arlington, Washington: Tilth, 1982.

US Department of Agriculture, *Report and Recommendations on Organic Farming*. Washington DC: USDA, 1980.

Business and the Workplace

These books challenge much of our thinking about the nature of work and work relationships. Hierarchical and authoritarian work environments are replaced by more democratic community-orientated approaches to work-related activities. Many of the alienating features, including the mind-body separation represented by scientific management, division of labor and specialization are challenged. New theories of work are based on the principles of re-integration of mind, body and spirit into the labor process.

Standard marketplace ideology is seen as inadequate because it can only take into consideration the time-span of the buyers and sellers presently involved in the marketplace. The new business philosophy broadens the production and consumption time-span to consider future generations in the decision making process.

Applegath, John, *Working Free*. New York: American Management Association, 1982.

Lievegoed, B.C.J., *The Developing Organization*. London: Tavistock, 1969.

Lindenfeld, F. and Rothschild-Whitt, Joyce, *Workplace Democracy and Social Change*. Boston: Porter Sargent Publishers, 1983.

Lippitt, Gordon, *Organization Renewal: A Holistic Approach to Organization Development*. Englewood Cliffs, NJ: Prentice-Hall, 1982.

Mares, William and Simmons, John, *Working Together: Participation from Shopfloor to Boardroom*. New York: Alfred Knopf, 1983.

Nightingale, Donald, *Workplace Democracy: An Inquiry into Employee Participation in Canadian Work Organizations*. University of Toronto Press, 1982.

Philips, Michael, *The Seven Laws of Money*. New York: Random House, 1974.

Resource Publishing Group, *Concerned Investors Guide; Non-Financial Corporate Data*. Arlington, VA: Resource Publishing Group, 1983.

Rifkin, Jeremy, *Own Your Own Job: Economic Democracy to Working Americans*. New York: Bantam Books, 1977.

Rifkin, Jeremy and Barber, Randy, *The North Will Rise Again*. Boston: Beacon Press, 1978.

——, et al., *Common Sense II: The Case Against Corporate Tyranny*. New York: Bantam, 1975.

Wilken, Folkert, *The Liberation of Work*. London: Routledge & Kegan Paul, 1969.

——, *The Liberation of Capital*. London: Allen & Unwin, 1982.

Work in America Institute, *Productivity Through Work Innovations*. Elsmford, New York: Pergamon, 1982.

Zager, R. and Rosow, M., eds, *Guide to New Work Innovations in America*. Elmsford, NY: Pergamon, 1982.

Ecology and Environmentalism

These books begin the process of introducing a new "deep ecology" ethos. They are all based on the critical need to balance our social consumption needs with the realities and limits of the natural production cycles.

Berg, Peter, *Reinhabiting a Separate Country: A Bioregional Anthology of Northern California*. CA: Planet Drum Foundation, 1978.
Clark, Wilson, *Energy for Survival*. New York: Doubleday/ Anchor Books, 1975.
Coates, Gary, ed., *Resettling America: Energy, Ecology and Community*. Andover, MA: Brick House, 1981.
Croner, Stan, *An Introduction to the World Conservation Strategy*. San Francisco: Friends of the Earth, 1983.
de Moll, Lane and Coe, Gigi, eds, *Stepping Stones: Appropriate Technology and Beyond*. New York: Schocken, 1978.
Goldsmith, E., et al., *Blueprint for Survival*. Signet, 1972.
Griffin, Susan, *Woman and Nature: The Roaring Inside Her*. San Francisco: Harper & Row, 1978.
Harding, Jim, et al., eds, *Tools for the Soft Path*. San Francisco: Friends of the Earth, 1982.
LaChapelle, Dolores, *Earth Wisdom*. Silverton, CO: Way of the Mountain Center, 1978.
Leopold, Aldo, *Sand County Almanac*. New York: Oxford University Press, 1968.
Lovins, Amory, *Soft Energy Paths*. London: Penguin, 1977.
Merrill, Richard and Gage, Thomas, eds, *Energy Primer: Solar, Water, Wind, and Biofuels*. New York: Delta, 1978.
Miller, G. Tyler, *Living in the Environment*, 3rd ed. Belmont, CA: Wadsworth, 1983.
Tobias, Michael, ed., *Deep Ecology*. San Diego, CA: Avant Books, 1985.
Todd, Nancy, ed., *The Book of the New Alchemists*. New York: Dutton, 1977.

Shelter

These books look at architecture and living environments from an integrated environmental perspective. The idea of space as a confining enclosure, cut off from the outside world, is replaced with the idea of structures as smaller communities embedded inside the larger biological and physical communities which make up the ecosystem. Structure as a spatial idea is replaced with the idea of structure as a temporal idea. The idea of walls and borders is replaced with the idea of structures as mediums to facilitate a rhythmic compatibility between inside and outside. Other values, beside strict efficiency, govern this new approach to architecture. These values include the resacralization of life in its various dimensions.

Corbett, Michael, *A Better Place to Live: New Designs for Tomorrow's Communities*. Emmaus, PA: Rodale Press, 1982.

Farallones Institute, *The Integral Urban House*. San Francisco: Sierra Club Books, 1979.

Soleri, Paolo, *The Bridge Between Matter and Spirit is Matter Becoming Spirit: The Arcology of Paolo Soleri*. New York: Anchor, 1973.

Todd, Nancy and Todd, Jack, *Bioshelters, Ocean Arks, City Farming: Ecology as the Basis of Design*. San Francisco: Sierra Club Books, 1984.